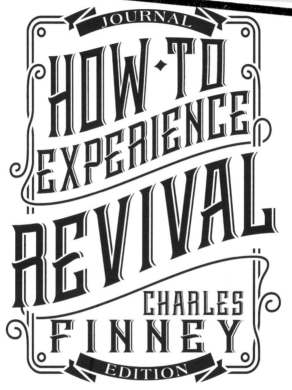

JOURNAL

HOW·TO
EXPERIENCE
REVIVAL

CHARLES
FINNEY

EDITION

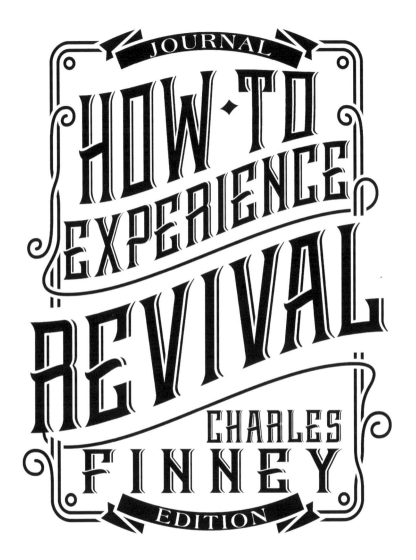

JOURNAL

HOW·TO EXPERIENCE

REVIVAL

CHARLES FINNEY

EDITION

W
WHITAKER
HOUSE

This new edition from Whitaker House has been updated for the modern reader. Words, expressions, and sentence structure have been revised for clarity and readability. Although the more modern Bible translations quoted in this edition were not available to the author, the Bible versions used were carefully selected in order to make the language of the entire text readily understandable while maintaining the author's original premises and message.

Unless otherwise indicated, Scripture quotations marked (NKJV) are taken from the *New King James Version*, © 1979, 1980, 1982 by Thomas Nelson, Inc. Used by permission. All rights reserved. Scripture quotations marked (KJV) are taken from the King James Version of the Bible.

How to Experience Revival
Journal Edition
This work is updated from *Finney on Revival* (London: Marshall Morgan and Scott, 1939), edited by E. E. Shelhamer, which was an abridgement of *Lectures on Revival* by Charles Finney (Fleming H. Revell, 1835). Previously published by Whitaker House as *How to Experience Revival* (1984) and *Experiencing Revival* (2004).

ISBN: 978-1-62911-785-0 • eBook ISBN: 978-1-62911-103-2
Printed in the United States of America
Copyright © 1984, 2017 by Whitaker House

Whitaker House
1030 Hunt Valley Circle
New Kensington, PA 15068
www.whitakerhouse.com

The Library of Congress has cataloged the original trade paperback edition as follows:

Finney, Charles Grandison, 1792–1875.
 Experiencing revival / by Charles Finney.
   p. cm.
 ISBN 0-88368-632-5
 1. Revivals. I. Title.
 BV3790 .F48 2000
 269'.24—dc21
                       00-010600

This book has been printed digitally and produced in a standard specification in order to ensure its continuing availability.

CONTENTS

NOTE FROM THE PUBLISHER

This new journal edition of Charles Finney's classic *How to Experience Revival* is specially designed to take you from words on a page to personal application and spiritual fruitfulness. In our age of distractions and hurry, many believers are reclaiming practices of meditation, of reflection, and of thoughtful prayer, as a way to connect with the things of God even while barraged by the things of this world. To that end, this journal edition was crafted. It invites the reader to meditate, reflect, and pray in response to the words of Finney's inspiring spiritual manual. Our hope is that engagement with the words and thoughts of a revivalist so close to the hand of God in a previous century will spark revival in our own.

ABOUT CHARLES FINNEY

Charles Finney (1792–1875) is known as the Father of Modern Revivalism, and for good reason. It has been said that more than a quarter of a million souls were converted under his fiery preaching. One of the leaders of the Second Great Awakening, Finney was a man with a message that burned through the religious deadwood and secular darkness of his time. He had the ability to shock saints and sinners alike. Radical in both his methods and his message, Finney was criticized for almost everything—except for being boring.

In one city where he spoke on eternal hellfire, a listener was so offended he came back to the second evening of the revival with a gun, planning to shoot Finney. Instead, that listener left converted. In another, a woman was struck speechless for sixteen hours from the work of the Spirit through Finney's preaching. Afterward, she admitted to Finney that she had thought she was saved before, but when truly presented with the righteousness of Christ, her heart was for the first time changed.

Born in Connecticut in 1792, Finney was nearly thirty years of age before he turned from his skepticism regarding Christianity and wholeheartedly embraced the Bible as the true Word of God. Ordained in 1824, he gave up his law profession in order to preach, but grew concerned when the members of his congregation repeatedly said they were "pleased" with his sermons. His preaching rapidly grew into the direct, explicit, and forceful calls-to-action and altar calls for which he is now famous.

While Finney carried his revivals to several Northeastern states, the bulk of his meetings were in New York towns, especially Rome, Rochester, Utica, Clinton, Antwerp, Evans' Mills, Western, and Gouverneur. In 1832, Finney began pastoring the Second Free Presbyterian Church in New York City. In 1835, he established the theology department at Oberlin Collegiate Institute in Oberlin, Ohio (known today as Oberlin College). He served there as a professor of theology as well as a pastor of Oberlin's First Congregational Church until a few years before his death. He was also a member of the Oberlin College Board of Trustees from 1846 until he was elected president of the college in 1851. During these years, he continued to carry on his evangelism, even visiting Great Britain twice in 1849–50 and 1859–60. In August of 1875, Finney died in Oberlin from a heart ailment.

Today, Charles Finney's legacy stretches far beyond Oberlin College, or even the cities in which he sparked revival. He is remembered as a vocal advocate for the abolition of slavery and for the equal education for men and women of all races. He is also considered by Christians worldwide as the forefather to evangelists Dwight L. Moody, Billy Sunday, and Billy Graham. His writings on the landmark revivals he labored for in the nineteenth century are classic expositions for all would-be revivalists and seekers of spiritual awakening in the twenty-first century and beyond.

PREFACE TO 1939 EDITION

The lectures of Charles Grandison Finney on religious revivals probably constitute the most exhaustive treatment of the subject that can be found. The lectures were the result of intense study, both of the Bible and of human need.

Finney was a highly spiritual and distinguished evangelist, pastor, and theologian, as well as the most noteworthy nineteenth-century apostle of revival. It is estimated that over 250,000 souls were converted as a result of his preaching.

In these busy days, many claim that there is little time to study the larger works that contain his complete messages. In this book, however, an attempt has been made to gather the main points and provide a handbook for Christians who wish to learn the simple principles of the promise of revival.

We often take it for granted that God's blessing will come in His own way and in His own good time. Finney, however, shows us that Scripture makes it plain that blessings follow when certain conditions are fulfilled in the hearts and lives of men. These essentials are set forth in this book, so that Finney's words may encourage this generation and inspire all who look for revival in our own time.

—*E. E. Shelhamer*

BEFORE YOU BEGIN

What is your definition of revival?

Renewal of this Christian Spirit. A
deeper sense of urgency to share the Gospel
of Jesus, both privately and cooperatively,
too bring back to life something
that is at the brink of death

Have you ever seen revival? If so, how did it manifest? How did it affect your life?

I have seen Revival meetings but
do not know if I've seen true
revival along the lines of my defination

Do you want revival today? If so, why and where?

Yes. First in my own heart then in the Community of FBCD.

WHEN TO EXPECT A REVIVAL

Will You not revive us again,
that Your people may rejoice in You?
—Psalm 85:6

When there is a lack of brotherly love and Christian confidence among believers, then a revival is needed. Then there is a loud call for God to revive His work.

Expect a revival when there are dissensions, jealousies, and evil rumors among believers. These things show that Christians have grown far away from God and that it is time to think seriously about a revival.

Revival is needed when there is a worldly spirit in the church. The church has sunk into a low and backslidden state when you see Christians conform to the world in dress, parties, seeking worldly amusement, and reading filthy novels.

When the church finds its members falling into gross and scandalous sins, then it is time to wake up and cry to God for a revival of religion.

ARE YOU A CARELESS CHRISTIAN?

When sinners are careless and stupid, it is time for Christians to get to work. It is as much their duty to wake up as it is for firemen to wake up when a fire breaks out. The church must put out the fires of hell that are consuming the wicked. Sleep? Should the firemen sleep and let the whole city burn down? What would people think of such firemen? And yet their guilt would not compare with the guilt of Christians who sleep while sinners around them are sinking into the fires of hell.

If a minister finds he has lost, in any degree, the confidence of his people, he should work for a revival, knowing that it is the only means of regaining their confidence. I do not mean that his motive should be merely to regain the confidence of his people, but a revival started through his initiative will restore the confidence of the praying group of his people. If an elder or private member of the church finds his brethren cold toward him, there is only one way to restore their faith. It is by being revived himself and pouring out the splendor of Jesus from his life.

The fact is, Christians are more to blame for not being revived than sinners are for not being converted.

KEEPING A CHURCH ALIVE

A church declining in this way cannot continue to exist without a revival. If it receives new members, they will, for the most part, be ungodly people. Without revivals, there usually will not even be as many people converted as die in a year. There have been churches in this country where all of the members have died off, and since there were no revivals to convert others to take their places, the church has died and the organization has dissolved.

Without a revival, sinners will grow harder and harder despite preaching. Your children and your friends will remain unsaved if there are no revivals to convert them. It would be better for them if there were no means of grace, no sanctuary, no Bible, and no preaching than to live and die where there is no revival.

There is no other way for a church to be sanctified, grow in grace, and be groomed for heaven. What is growing in grace? Is it hearing sermons and getting some new ideas about religion? No, not at all. The Christian who does this, and nothing else, will grow worse and worse, more and more hardened. Finally, it will be nearly impossible to rouse him.

THE SPIRIT OF PRAYER

A revival can be expected when Christians have the spirit of prayer for a revival—that is, when they pray as if their hearts were set on it. Sometimes, Christians do not use a definite prayer for a revival, even when they are inspired in prayer. Their minds are on something else—the salvation of the lost—and they are not praying for a revival among themselves. But when they feel the lack of a revival, they will pray for it. People feel for their own families and neighborhoods, so they will earnestly pray for them.

What constitutes the spirit of prayer? Is it fervent words and many prayers? No. Prayer is the state of the heart. The spirit of prayer is a state of continual desire and anxiety for the salvation of sinners. It can even be something that weighs a person down. It is the same, as far as the philosophy of mind is concerned, as when a person is concerned with some worldly interest. A Christian who has this spirit of prayer feels concerned for souls. They are always on his mind. He thinks of them by day and dreams of them by night. This is "praying without ceasing." (See 1 Thessalonians 5:17.) His prayers seem to flow from his heart like water: *"O Lord, revive Your work"* (Habakkuk 3:2). Sometimes this feeling is very deep.

This is by no means <u>fanaticism.</u> It is just what Paul felt when he said, *"My little children, for whom I labor in birth"* (Galatians 4:19). This labor of soul is that deep agony that people feel when they hold on to God for a blessing and will not let Him go until they receive it. I do not mean to say that it is essential to have this great distress in order to have the spirit of prayer. But the deep, continual, earnest desire for the salvation of sinners is what constitutes the spirit of prayer for a revival.

REVIVAL *riviva a spirit of service in Me*

_____

_____

_____

_____

_____

THE HOLY SPIRIT'S ROLE IN REVIVAL

When this desire exists in a church, unless the Spirit is grieved away by sin, there will always be a revival of Christians. Generally, it will involve the conversion of sinners to Jesus. A clergyman once told me of a revival among his people that started with a zealous and devoted woman in the church. She became concerned about sinners and started praying for them. She prayed, and her distress increased.

She finally went to her minister and talked with him, asking him to schedule an evangelistic meeting. She felt that one was needed. The minister put her off because he did not feel the same need. The next week she came again, asking him to schedule a meeting. She knew people would come because she felt God was going to pour out His Spirit. The minister put her off once more.

Finally, she said to him, "If you do not schedule the meeting, I will die, because there is going to be a revival." The next Sunday, he scheduled a meeting. He said that if anyone wished to talk with him about the salvation of his soul, he would meet with him. He did not know of anyone who was concerned over his soul, but when he went to the appointed place, he was surprised to find a large number of anxious inquirers.

Do you think that woman knew there was going to be a revival? Call it what you like, a new revelation or an old revelation or anything else. It was the Spirit of God who showed that praying woman there was going to be a revival. The secret of the Lord was with her, and she knew it. She knew God had been in her heart and had filled it so full that she could not hold it in.

CONFESSION, SACRIFICE, DETERMINATION

A revival is near when Christians begin to confess their sins to one another. Usually they confess in a general, halfhearted manner. They may do it in eloquent language, but it means nothing. But when there is an honest breaking down and a pouring out of the heart in confession of sin, the floodgates will soon burst open, and salvation will flow everywhere.

A revival can be expected when Christians are willing to make the sacrifices necessary to carry it on. They must be willing to sacrifice their feelings, business, and time to help the work.

Ministers must be willing to expend their energy. They must be willing to offend the impenitent by plain and faithful speech and perhaps offend many members of the church who will not repent. They must take a stand regarding the revival, whatever the consequences. They must be prepared to go on with the work even though they risk losing the affection of the impenitent and cold members of the church. The minister must be prepared, if it is the will of God, to be driven away from the place. He must be determined to go straight forward, leaving the event in God's hands.

SACRIFICE _____

_____

_____

_____

_____

_____

I knew a minister who had a young man working with him on a revival. The young man preached the plain truth, and the wicked did not like him. They said, "We like our minister, and we want to have him preach." They finally complained so much that the minister told the young man, "Such and such a person, who gives so much money for support, says so-and-so; Mr. A. also says so, and Mr. B. likewise. They think it will break up the church if you continue to preach, and I think you had better not preach anymore."

The young man left, but the Spirit of God immediately withdrew from the place and the revival stopped. The minister, by yielding to the wicked desires of the ungodly, drove the Spirit away. The minister was afraid that the devil would drive him away from his people. So, by trying to satisfy the devil, he offended God. And God so ordered events that in a short time the minister had to leave his people after all. The minister tried to go between the devil and God, and God dismissed him.

REFLECTION ON...

Expecting Revival _____

_____

_____

_____

_____

_____

PREPARING THE HEART FOR REVIVAL

*Break up your fallow ground, for it is time to seek the LORD,
till He comes and rains righteousness on you.*
—Hosea 10:12

Because the Jews were a nation of farmers, Scripture often refers to their occupation to illustrate its points. The prophet Hosea employed this strategy to tell the Jews they were becoming a nation of backsliders. He reproved them for their idolatry and threatened them with the judgments of God.

A revival consists of two parts: that which concerns the church and that which concerns the unsaved. Here I will speak about a revival in the church. Fallow ground is ground that has once been tilled but that now lies waste. It needs to be broken up and mellowed before it is again ready to receive grain.

SOFTENING YOUR HEART

If you want to break up the fallow ground of your heart, you must begin by looking at yourself. Examine and note the state of your mind. See where you are. Many people never seem to think about this. They pay no attention to their own hearts, and they never know whether they are doing well in their faith or not. They do not know whether they are gaining ground or going back, whether they are fruitful or going to waste.

Now is the time to divert your attention from other things and look into this. Make a point to do this. Do not be in a hurry. Thoroughly examine the state of your heart and see where you are. Check to see if you are walking with God every day or with the devil.

Self-examination is looking at your life. It is considering your actions in the past and learning the true character of your life. Look over your personal history. Examine your individual sins one by one. I do not mean for you to glance at your past life, see that it has been full of sins, then go to God and make a general confession. That is not the way. You must look at each sin one by one. It is a good idea to take a pen and paper as you go over them and write each sin down as it occurs to you.

Go over them as carefully as a merchant goes over his books. Each time a sin comes to mind, add it to the list. General confessions of sin will never do. Your sins were committed one by one, and they should be reviewed and repented of one by one. Now, begin and review what are commonly, but improperly, called sins of omission.

OUR NEGLECT

Ingratitude

Write down under this heading all the times you can remember when you have received favors from God for which you have never thanked Him. How many cases can you remember? Perhaps you remember a remarkable provision, some wonderful turn of events that saved you from ruin. Write down the instances of God's goodness to you when you were in sin—before your conversion—for which you have never been thankful enough. Do not forget the numerous mercies you have received since. How long is the list of times when your ingratitude has been so lacking that you want to hide your face in shame?

Go down on your knees, confess these times one by one to God, and ask forgiveness. The very act of confession, by the laws of suggestion, will bring similar sins to mind. Write these down. Review them three or four times this same way and see what an astonishing number of mercies there are for which you have never thanked God.

Ingratitude _____

_____

_____

_____

_____

Lack of Love for God

Think how grieved and alarmed you would be if you discovered any lessening of affection for you in your wife, husband, or children. If you saw another engrossing their hearts, thoughts, and time, wouldn't you be hurt? Perhaps, in such a case, you would feel you would die of a just and virtuous jealousy. In a similar way,

God calls Himself a jealous God. (See Exodus 20:5.) Have you not given your heart to other loves and infinitely offended Him?

LACK OF LOVE FOR GOD _____

Neglecting Your Bible Reading

Note the cases when, for perhaps weeks or longer, reading God's Word was not a pleasure. Some people read whole chapters so carelessly that they cannot remember what they have been reading. If so, no wonder your life is without purpose and your religion is such a miserable failure.

Also note instances of unbelief. Recall the times when you have virtually charged the God of truth with lying by your unbelief in His promises and declarations. God has promised to give the Holy Spirit to those who ask Him. (See Luke 11:13.) Now, do you believe this? Have you expected Him to answer? Have you not virtually said in your hearts, when you prayed for the Holy Spirit, "I do not believe that I will receive"? If you have not believed or expected to receive the blessing that God has specifically promised, you have accused Him of lying.

BIBLE READING _____

_____

_____

_____

_____

_____

Neglect of Prayer

Think of the times when you have neglected secret prayer, family prayer, and prayer meetings. Remember when you have prayed in such a way that offended God more than if you had omitted prayer altogether.

PRAYER _____

_____

_____

_____

_____

_____

Poor Spiritual Attitude

The way you have performed your spiritual duties can also reflect a poor attitude. For example, a person can pray with a lack of feeling or faith, in a worldly frame of mind, so that his words are nothing but mere chatter. Someone who prays this kind of lifeless, careless prayer would not be able to give a reason for his or her prayers.

REFLECTION ON...

SPIRITUAL ATTITUDE _____

_____

_____

_____

_____

A Lack of Love for the Souls of Others

Look at your friends and relatives and remember how little compassion you have felt for them. You have stood by and watched them going right to hell, yet it seemed as though you did not care. How many days have there been in which you failed to pray about their sinful condition or show any ardent desire for their salvation?

LACK OF LOVE _____

_____

_____

_____

_____

_____

_____

A Lack of Concern for Unbelievers

Perhaps you have not cared enough for unbelievers to attempt to learn about their condition. Perhaps you will not even subscribe to a missionary magazine. Look at these factors and see how much you really care for the lost. Write down your true concern for them and your desire for their salvation. Measure your desire for their salvation. Measure it by the self-denial you practice to help send them the gospel.

LACK OF CONCERN _____

_____

_____

_____

_____

_____

Sin of Hypocrisy

Do you deny yourself the luxuries of life? Do you economize, or are you unwilling to subject yourself to any inconvenience to save the lost? Do you pray for them daily in private? Are you praying with the correct attitude? If you are not doing these things, and if your soul is not agonized for the unsaved, why are you such a hypocrite pretending to be a Christian? Your practice of faith is an insult to Jesus Christ!

HYPOCRISY _____

_____

_____

_____

_____

_____

Neglect of Family and Private Duties

Think of how you have lived, putting yourself before your family. How have you prayed? What example have you set before them? What direct efforts do you habitually make for their spiritual good? What duties have you neglected?

Are you watchful of your own life? Think of how you have hurried through your private duties, never really checking yourself or keeping your accounts straight with God. How often have you entirely neglected to watch your conduct, and having been off your guard, sinned before the world, the church, and God?

YOUR DUTIES _____

_____

_____

_____

_____

_____

Neglecting to Watch Over Fellow Believers

It is wrong to neglect to watch over your brothers and sisters in Christ. How often have you broken your covenant to watch over them in the Lord? How little do you know or care about the state of their souls? Yet you are under a solemn oath to watch over them. What have you done to become acquainted with them? With how many of them have you taken enough interest to know their spiritual states? Go over the list and wherever you find there has been neglect, write it down.

How many times have you seen your fellow believers growing cold in faith and not spoken to them about it? You have seen them beginning to neglect one duty after another, and you did not reprove them in a loving way. You have seen them falling into sin, and you let them go on. Yet you pretend to love them. What a hypocrite! Would you watch your spouse or child go into disgrace, or fall into the fire, and hold your peace? No, you would not. What do you think of yourself, then, when you pretend to love Christians (and Christ) while you watch your brothers and sisters fall into disgrace without saying anything?

W ATCHING OVER OTHERS _____

_____

_____

_____

_____

_____

Neglect of Self-Denial

There are many who are willing to do almost anything in religion as long as it does not require self-denial. When they are required to do anything that requires them to deny themselves, that is asking too much! They think they are doing a lot for God, as much as He can reasonably ask. They are unwilling to deny themselves any comfort or convenience for the sake of serving the Lord. They will not willingly suffer disgrace for the name of Jesus Christ. Nor will they deny themselves the luxuries of life to save a world from hell.

They have no idea that self-denial is a condition of discipleship. They do not even know what self-denial is. They have never really denied themselves even a trinket for Christ and the gospel. Some give great sums of money, and they do not feel the loss because their offering comes out of their surplus. These people often have the audacity to complain about others who give less than they. Yet those about whom they complain may be giving out of what they need. The poor woman who puts in her dollar has shown more self-denial than they have in giving thousands.

Self-denial _____

_____

_____

_____

_____

_____

ACTIVE SIN CHOICES

Worldliness

What has been the state of your heart in regard to your worldly possessions? Have you looked at them as really yours—as if you had a right to dispose of them as your own, according to your own will? If you have, write that down. If you have loved property and sought after it for its own sake to gratify lust, ambition, a worldly spirit, or to lay it up for your family, you have sinned. You must repent.

WORLDLINESS _____

_____

_____

_____

_____

Pride

Remember all the instances you can when you have found yourself acting or thinking with pride. Vanity is a particular form of pride. How many times have you been vain about your dress and appearance?

How many times have you thought more about and taken more trouble and time decorating your body to go to church than preparing your mind to worship God? When you have attended church, you have cared more about how you appeared physically to other people than how your soul appeared to the heart-searching God.

You have, in fact, set yourself up to be worshipped by others, rather than to worship God yourself. You sought to divide the worship of God's house, to draw the attention of God's people to your outward appearance. Do not pretend that you do not care anything about having people look at you. Be honest about it! Would you take all this time with your looks if every person were blind?

REFLECTION ON...

PRIDE _____

_____

_____

_____

_____

_____

Envy

Look at the times when you were envious of those who you thought were above you in any way. Perhaps you have envied those who are more talented or more useful than yourself. Have you not so envied some people that you could not stand to hear them praised? It has been more pleasant to you to dwell on their faults rather than their virtues, their failures rather than their successes. Be honest with yourself. If you have harbored this spirit of hell, repent deeply before God, or He will never forgive you.

ENVY _____

_____

_____

_____

_____

_____

A Critical Spirit

Remember the times you have had a bitter spirit and spoken of Christians in a manner that did not show charity or love. Love requires you to hope the best that a situation will permit and believe the best about any questionable conduct.

CRITICAL SPIRIT _____

_____

_____

_____

_____

_____

Slander

The times you have spoken unnecessarily about the faults, real or imagined, of members of the church or others behind their backs—this is slander. You do not need to lie to be guilty of slander. Telling the truth with the intent to injure is slander.

SLANDER _____

_____

_____

_____

_____

Lack of Respect

How often have you been lighthearted before God as you would not have dared to be in the presence of an earthly ruler? Perhaps you have been an atheist and forgotten that there is a God. Or perhaps you have had less respect for Him and His presence than you would show toward an earthly judge.

DISRESPECT _____

_____

_____

_____

_____

Lying

Understand what lying is. It is any kind of intended deception. If the deception is not intentional, it is not lying. But if you decide to make an impression contrary to the naked truth, you lie. Write down all those incidents you can remember. Do not call them by any soft names. God calls them lies and charges you with lying. You, too, must charge yourself correctly. How numerous are the falsehoods perpetuated every day in business, social situations, words, looks, and actions! All are designed to make an impression on others for selfish reasons that are contrary to the truth!

LYING _____

_____

_____

_____

_____

Cheating

Remember all the cases in which you have dealt with an individual and done to him what you would not like to have done to you. That is cheating. God has laid down a rule for this case: *"Whatever you want men to do to you, do also to them"* (Matthew 7:12). That is the rule. And if you have not followed this rule, you are a cheat. Notice that the rule is not that you should do "what you might reasonably expect them to do to you," because that is a rule that would permit every degree of wickedness. But it is *"whatever you want men to do to you."*

CHEATING_____

_____

_____

_____

_____

_____

Hypocrisy

Hypocrisy may exist in your prayers and confessions to God. Remember when you have prayed for things you did not really want. You will know this is happening if, when you have finished praying, you cannot remember exactly what you have prayed for. How many times have you confessed sins that you did not mean to stop committing? Yes, you confessed sins when you knew you would repeat them, just as you expected to continue living.

HYPOCRISY _____

_____

_____

_____

_____

_____

Robbing God

Think of the times you have misspent your time, squandering the hours that God gave you to serve Him and save souls. Maybe you spend too much time with idle pastimes, more than working to bring people to Jesus. Maybe you do absolutely nothing. Think of cases where you have misapplied your talents and mental powers. Where have you squandered money on your lusts, or spent it for things that you did not need and that did not contribute to your health, comfort, or usefulness?

ROBBING GOD_____

_____

_____

_____

_____

_____

Bad Temper

Perhaps you have abused your spouse, children, family, coworkers, or neighbors. Write it all down.

ANGER_____

_____

_____

_____

_____

_____

Hindering Others from Being Useful

Perhaps you have weakened another Christian's influence by insinuations against him. You have not only robbed God of your own talents, but also tied the hands of somebody else. What a wicked person is he who not only wastes time himself, but also hinders others! This is done sometimes by taking their time needlessly, sometimes by destroying Christian confidence in them. By doing these things, you have played into the hands of Satan, and you have not only proved yourself to be an idle vagabond, but also prevented others from working.

_____

_____

_____

_____

_____

REMOVING ROADBLOCKS TO
INCREASED FAITH

If you find you have committed a fault against an individual, and that individual is within your reach, go confess it immediately and get that transgression out of the way. If the individual you have injured is too far away for you to go and see him, write a letter confessing the injury. If you have defrauded anybody, return his money in full with interest.

Get to work with your restitution now! Go now! Do not put it off. Procrastination will only make the matter worse. Confess to God those sins that have been committed against Him. Confess to man those sins that have been committed against him. Don't think you can get out of this obligation by ignoring the old stumbling blocks on your road of life. In breaking up your fallow ground, you must remove every obstruction. Things may be left that you think are insignificant. However, if you do not remove the obstacles and do your best to make restitution for your mistakes, you will not feel at peace. The reason for the lack of joy in your relationship with Jesus is that your proud and carnal mind has covered up something that God required you to confess and remove.

FRUITFUL A HUNDREDFOLD

Break up all the ground and turn it over. Do not balk; do not turn away because of little difficulties. Drive the plow right through them. Go deep and turn the ground up so that it will all be mellow and soft. Then it will be ready to receive the seed and bear fruit a hundredfold.

When you have thoroughly gone over your whole history in this way, go over the ground a second time, paying special attention to it. You will find the things you put down will suggest other sins of which you have been guilty. These new ones are usually connected with the original offenses. Then go over it a third time, and you will remember other things. You will find, in the end, that you can remember particular actions that you did not think you would remember even in eternity.

Unless you consider your sins in this way—in detail, one by one—you cannot comprehend their number. You should go over this list as thoroughly, carefully, and seriously as you would if you were preparing yourself for the Final Judgment.

As you go over the catalog of your sins, make a resolution to reform your ways now. Wherever you find anything wrong, resolve at once, in the strength of God, to sin no more in that way. It will not benefit you to examine yourself unless you decide to change every fault you find in your heart, temper, and conduct.

_____

_____

_____

_____

_____

HOW SIN BLOCKS JOY

If, as you proceed with this project, you find that your spirit is still not rejoicing, search yourself. You will see that there is still sin blocking your full awareness of the Spirit of God within you. This lack of joy is your signal that you have not been faithful and thorough. Your self-examination requires a full attack—it is not a gentle pastime. It is tearing sin away from yourself, revealing what can be painful.

You must honestly look at yourself, using your Bible as your checkpoint. Do not expect God to miraculously break up your fallow ground for you. You must actively participate, and you must submit your will. If you look at yourself accurately, taking note of your sins, you will definitely feel something. You cannot see your sins for what they are without deeply feeling something.

Experience proves the benefit of going over our histories in this way. Start your work now. Resolve that you will not stop until you find you can pray. You will never have access to the full power of the Holy Spirit dwelling within you unless you completely confess your sins. Let there be this deep work of repentance and full confession, this breaking down before God.

Then you will have as much of the spirit of prayer as you can tolerate. The reason so few Christians know anything about the spirit of prayer is that they never take the trouble to examine themselves properly, and so they never know what it is to have their hearts broken up to be rebuilt in this way.

CONFESSION _____

_____

_____

_____

_____

_____

OUTWARD ACTIVITY AND FRUITLESS CHRISTIANS

It will do no good to preach to you while your heart is in this hardened, fallow state. The farmer might just as well sow his grain on the rock, because it will not bring forth fruit. This is why there are so many fruitless believers in the church—why there is so much outward activity yet so little profound feeling.

Look at the Sunday school, for instance, and see how much activity there is and how little Christian spirit. If you continue this way, the work will continue to harden you. You will grow worse and worse, just as the rain and snow on an old fallow field make the turf thicker and the clods stronger.

FRUITFULNESS _____

_____

_____

_____

_____

_____

WHEN REVIVAL STARTS

Those who profess to be Christians should never be so self-satisfied that they expect to start a revival by suddenly jumping out of their sleep, blustering about, and talking to sinners. They must break up their own fallow ground. If your fallow ground is broken up, then the way to get more zest is to go out and see sinners on the road to hell, talk to them, and guide inquiring souls.

You may get excited without this breaking up of your fallow ground. You may show a kind of zeal, but it will not last long, and it will not take hold of sinners, unless your heart is broken up. Unless you are right with God and filled with the Spirit, your work will be mechanical and fruitless.

And now, will you break up your fallow ground? Will you clear your heart before God and persevere until you are thoroughly awake? If you fail here, if you do not do this, you will not get any further. I have gone as far with you as possible until you renew your neglected spiritual life.

Without a heart ready to receive the fullness of Jesus again, the rest of this book is worthless to the reader. It will only harden you and make you worse. If you do not start working on your heart immediately, one can say that you have no intention of being revived; you have forsaken your minister, letting him fight the battle alone. If you do not do this, I charge you with having forsaken Christ, with refusing to repent and work for Him.

PREPARING YOUR HEART FOR REVIVAL

THE SPIRIT OF PRAYER

*Likewise the Spirit also helps in our weaknesses. For we
do not know what we should pray for as we ought, but the
Spirit Himself makes intercession for us with groanings
which cannot be uttered. Now He who searches the hearts
knows what the mind of the Spirit is, because He makes
intercession for the saints according to the will of God.*
—Romans 8:26–27

We are ignorant of both the will of God as revealed in the Bible and the unrevealed will of God as we can learn it from His providence. Mankind is also vastly ignorant of the promises and prophesies in the Bible. We are even more in the dark about those points God gives us through the leadings of His Spirit.

I have named these four reasons to ground our faith in prayer: providences, promises, prophecies, and the Holy Spirit. When all other means fail to lead us to pray for the right things, the Spirit does it.

I once knew an individual who was in great spiritual darkness. He went off by himself to pray, resolving that he would not stop until he found the Lord. This man knelt down and tried to pray. His mind was dark, and he could not pray. He got up from his knees and stood awhile, but he could not give up because he had promised he would not let the sun go down before he gave himself to God. He knelt again, but his heart was as dark and hard as before. He was nearly in despair, and he said in agony, "I have grieved the Spirit of God away, and there is no hope for me. I am shut out from the presence of God."

HOW TO FIND HIM

But he was resolved not to give up. Again he knelt down. He had said only a few words when this passage came to mind, as fresh as if he had just read it: *"You will seek Me and find Me, when you search for Me with all your heart"* (Jeremiah 29:13). He saw that though this promise was in the Old Testament, and addressed to the Jews, it was as applicable to him as to them. His hard heart broke when the Lord Himself hammered it with this Scripture. This young man prayed and then got up to leave, filled with the joy of Jesus.[1]

---

1. In this passage, Finney uses the Pauline expression, *"I knew a man"* (2 Corinthians 12:2) to tell the story of his own conversion. It occurred at Adams, New York, where he was studying law. In his study of the Bible, he had come under deepening conviction, realizing that "salvation, instead of being a thing to be brought about by my own works, was a thing to be found entirely in the Lord Jesus, who presented Himself as my God and my Savior." As he walked along the street, an inward voice seemed to demand, "Will you accept it now, today?" His reply was, "Yes, I will accept it today, or I will die trying." Instead of going on to his studies, he made his way into the woods near the village and crept between some fallen trees to pray. There, as he said afterward, "God gave me many other promises in addition to the text quoted from Jeremiah, especially some very precious promises regarding our Lord Jesus Christ. I seized them." His disquieted mind became "wonderfully calm and peaceful." He thought, as he walked back toward Adams, "My mind was so perfectly quiet that it seemed as if all nature listened." He had gone to the woods immediately after an early breakfast, and by this time it was dinnertime. Yet it appeared to him that he had been absent only a little while. —E. E. Shelhamer [See Finney's *Holy Spirit Revivals* (New Kensington, PA: Whitaker House, 1999).]

INTERCESSORY PRAYER

I was acquainted with a pastor who used to keep a list of people for whom he was especially concerned, and I have had the opportunity to know a multitude of people who were immediately converted after he began praying for them. I have seen him pray literally in agony for the people on this list. At times he would call on another Christian to help him pray for someone. His mind would become intensely fixed in prayer upon an individual who had a hardened, abandoned character, and who could not be reached in any ordinary way.

In one town where there was a revival, there was an individual who violently opposed Christianity. He ran a tavern and delighted in swearing whenever there were Christians within hearing distance. He was so bad that one man said he would either have to sell his place or give it away because he could not stand to live near a man who swore like that.

When this praying pastor passed through the town and heard of the case, he was very distressed for the individual, and he put the curser on his prayer list. The case weighed on his mind when he was asleep as well as when he was awake. He continued thinking about the ungodly man and praying for him for days. Not long afterward, the tavern keeper came to a meeting and confessed his sins. He poured out his soul, and he seemed to be one of the most repentant men ever seen. His testimony seemed to cover the whole ground of his treatment of God, Christians, the revival, and everything good. This new convert's bar immediately became the place where they held prayer meetings.[2]

---

2. In remarkable contrast, there was the case of a railing infidel who, in the middle of his discourse, suffered a stroke. A physician assured him that he did not have long to live, and that if he had anything to say, he must say it at once. He had only time and strength to stammer out one sentence. It was, "Don't let Finney pray over my corpse." —E. E. Shelhamer

The Spirit of God leads individual Christians to pray in this manner for things that they would not pray for without being led by the Spirit. In this way, they pray for things *"according to the will of God"* (Romans 8:27).

INTERCESSORY PRAYER _____

_____

_____

_____

_____

_____

_____

_____

THE LEADING OF THE SPIRIT

A lot of harm has been done by those who say that this leading by the Spirit is a new revelation. Calling this leading a revelation has caused many people to be apprehensive of it. The strength of the term has frightened them so that they will not even stop to see what revelation means or if the Bible even teaches the principle.

The plain truth of the matter is that the Spirit leads a man to pray. If God leads a man to pray for an individual, the inference from the Bible is that God plans to save that individual. If we find, by comparing our state of mind with the Bible, that we are led by the Spirit to pray for an individual, we have solid evidence to believe that God is prepared to bless him. Devoted, praying Christians often see these things so clearly, and look so far ahead, that they confuse others. They sometimes almost seem to prophesy.

Undoubtedly, many people think they are being led by the Spirit when in fact they are leaning on their own understanding. But there is no doubt that a Christian may be enabled to clearly discern the signs of the times so as to understand, by providence, what to expect, and to pray for it in faith. Believers are often led to expect a revival and to pray for it in faith, when nobody else can see the least sign of it.

UNDERSTANDING GOD'S DIRECTION

There was a woman living in a New Jersey town where there had just been a revival. She was positive there was going to be another. She wanted to arrange conference meetings, but the minister and elders saw nothing to encourage a revival, so they did nothing. She saw they were blind, so she got a carpenter to make seats for her house where she would have the meetings. There was certainly going to be a revival!

She had scarcely opened her doors for meetings when the Spirit of God came down with great power, and these sleepy Christians found themselves surrounded, all at once, with convicted sinners. They could only say, "*Surely the LORD is in this place, and* [we] *did not know it*" (Genesis 28:16).

People like this woman understand the direction of God's will because the Spirit of God leads them to the understanding, not because they are so wise. The Lord's wisdom shows them how events are all leading to a particular result.

As the Scripture text at the beginning of this chapter says, *"The Spirit Himself makes intercession for us with groanings which cannot be uttered."* The meaning of this, as I understand it, is that the Spirit excites desires too great to be uttered except by groans—making the soul too full to utter its feelings by words. The person can only groan them out to God, who understands the language of the heart.

How is a sinner to get conviction? By thinking of his sins. That is also the way for a Christian to gain a deep awareness— by thinking about the subject. God is not going to pour these things on you without any effort of your own. You must cherish the slightest impressions. Take the Bible and go over the passages that show the conditions and prospects of the world. Look at the world, your children, and your neighbors and see their condition while they remain in sin. Then, persevere in prayer and effort until you obtain the blessing of the Spirit of God.

I have spent much time on this subject because I want it to be plain to you so that you will be careful not to grieve the Spirit. I want you to have high ideas of the Holy Spirit and to recognize that nothing good will be done without His influences. No praying or preaching will make any difference without Him. If Jesus Christ were to come down here and preach to sinners, not one would be converted without the Spirit. Be careful, then, not to grieve Him by slighting or neglecting His heavenly influences when He invites you to pray.

GOD'S DIRECTION _____

_____

_____

_____

_____

_____

PRAYER FORMS

We see from this subject the absurdity of using set prayers or prayer books. The very idea of using a form rejects the leading of the Spirit. Nothing is more calculated to destroy the spirit of prayer, and entirely darken and confuse the mind to what constitutes prayer, than prayer forms. Rote prayers are not only absurd in themselves, but they are the very device of the devil to destroy the spirit and break the power of prayer.

Prayer does not consist of mere words. It does not matter what the words are if the heart is not led by the Spirit of God. If the desire is not kindled, the thoughts directed, and the whole current of feeling produced and led by the Spirit of God, it is not prayer. Set forms keep an individual from praying as he could.

EXPERIENCING THE SPIRIT OF PRAYER

"The Spirit Himself makes intercession." For whom does He pray? For the saints! If you are a believer, you know by experience what it is to be exercised like this. Or, if you do not, it is because

you have grieved the Spirit of God so that He will not lead you. You probably have not yet experienced His filling. You live in such a manner that this holy Comforter will not make His presence known with you or give you the spirit of prayer.

If this is so, you must repent. Do not stop to decide whether you are a Christian or not, but repent as if you have never repented. Do not take it for granted that you are a Christian, but go like a humble sinner and pour out your heart to the Lord. You can never have the spirit of prayer in any other way. Nothing will produce more excitement and opposition than the spirit of prayer.

THE SPIRIT OF PRAYER

PREVAILING PRAYER

*The effective, fervent prayer of a righteous
man avails much.*
—James 5:16

There are two goals necessary for a revival: one is to influence men, and the other is to influence God. The truth is employed to influence men, and prayer is employed to move God. When I speak of moving God, I do not mean that God's mind is changed by prayer or that His disposition or character is changed. Prayer produces such a change in us that God is completely consistent with His nature when He answers our prayers.

When a sinner repents, his state of feeling makes it proper for God to forgive him. God has always been ready to forgive men on that condition. Therefore, when the sinner changes his feelings and repents, it requires no change of feeling in God to pardon him. It is the sinner's repentance that renders His forgiveness proper. This is when God will act.

Some people don't make the mistake of overemphasizing the role of prayer in "changing" God's mind, but they overlook the fact that prayer could be offered forever, by itself, apart from the work of the Holy Spirit, and nothing would be accomplished.

SPECIFIC PRAYERS

Many people go to their rooms alone "to pray," simply because "they must say their prayers." The time of day has come when they are in the habit of praying—in the morning, at noon, or at whatever time of day it may be. But instead of having anything to say, any definite reason on their minds, they fall down on their knees and simply pray for whatever floats into their imaginations. When they have finished, they can hardly remember what they have been praying for. This is not effective prayer.

To pray effectively, you must pray with submission to the will of God. Do not confuse submission with indifference. No two things are more unlike. I once knew an individual who came to a revival. He was cold and did not enter into the spirit of prayer. When he heard believers praying as if they could not be denied, he was shocked at their boldness. He insisted on the importance of praying with submission. Yet it was plain that he confused submission with indifference.

CRUCIAL PRAYER

If the will of God is not known, submission without prayer is tempting God. For all you know, your prayer may be the thing on which an event turns. In the case of an impenitent friend, your prayers may be the key to his being saved.

Christians often amaze themselves when they look back on their ardent, bold prayers spoken in a moment of intense emotion. Yet these prayers have prevailed and obtained the blessing. And many of these people are among the holiest people I know in the world.

SUBMISSIVE PRAYER_____

_____

_____

_____

_____

_____

EFFECTIVE MOTIVES

The temptation to have selfish motives is so strong that there is reason to fear that a great many parental prayers never rise above the yearnings of parental tenderness. That is why so many prayers are not answered and why so many pious, praying parents have ungodly children. Prayer for the unsaved must be based on more than sympathy. Missionaries and others often make the mistake of praying only about those going to hell, forgetting prayer about how the unsaved also dishonor God.

Most Christians work up to prevailing prayer through a prolonged process. Their minds gradually become filled with anxiety about something, until they even go about their business sighing out their desires to God. It is like the mother whose child is sick who constantly sighs as if her heart would break. If she is a praying mother, her sighs are breathed out to God all day long. If she leaves the room where her child is, her mind is still on her baby. If she is asleep, her thoughts are still on her child. She will even jerk in her dreams, thinking that perhaps her child may be dying. Her whole mind is absorbed with that sick child. This is the state of mind in which Christians offer prevailing prayer.

MOTIVES_____

_____

_____

_____

_____

_____

THE DEPTH OF CONCERN

The spirit of those who have been in distress for the souls of others is similar to that of the apostle Paul, who worked for souls and was ready to wish himself cut off from Christ for the sake of others. (See Romans 9:1–3.)

The psalmist showed the same concern when he prayed, *"Indignation has taken hold of me because of the wicked, who forsake Your law.… Rivers of water run down from my eyes, because men do not keep Your law"* (Psalm 119:53, 136). The prophet Jeremiah also experienced great sorrow because of Israel's sins. *"O my soul, my soul! I am pained in my very heart! My heart makes a noise in me; I cannot hold my peace, because you have heard, O my soul, the sound of the trumpet, the alarm of war"* (Jeremiah 4:19). In view of this, why should people be considered crazy if they cannot help but cry out loud when they think of the misery of those who are going to eternal destruction?

If you plan to pray effectively, you must pray a lot. It was said of the apostle James that, after his death, people noticed his knees were calloused, like a camel's, from praying so much. Ah, here was the secret of the success of those first ministers! They had calloused knees!

He spent his waking hours on his knees for those lost souls Aaron nim

USING THE NAME

If you intend to pray effectively, you must offer your prayers in the name of Christ. You cannot come to God in your own name. You cannot plead your own merits. But you can come in a name that is always acceptable. You know what it is to use the name of a man. If you were to go to the bank with a check endorsed by a millionaire (which would be the equivalent of his giving you his name), you know you could get the money from the bank as easily as he could. In the same way, Jesus Christ gives you the use of His name. When you pray in the name of Christ, you can prevail just as well as He and receive just as much as God's beloved Son would if He were to pray for the same things. You must pray in faith.

These strong desires behind the prevailing prayer I mentioned are the natural results of great benevolence and a clear view of the danger for sinners. This is a reasonable sentiment. If the average Christian were to see a home burning, hear the shrieks of the family inside, and see their agony, he or she would be extremely upset—perhaps even sick. No one would consider these reactions strange. In fact, if they had no powerful reaction, they would be considered coldhearted.

THE NECESSITY OF A LOVING CHARACTER

Why is it, then, that Christians are thought of as lunatics for their concern about the awful danger sinners are in? The fact is, those individuals who have never felt such concern have never felt real benevolence and must have a very superficial Christian love. I do not mean to judge harshly or speak unkindly, but it is a simple fact that a person without such a loving character is a superficial believer. This is not being critical; it is the plain truth.

When Christians are driven to the extreme, they make a desperate effort and roll the burden on the Lord Jesus Christ. They exercise a childlike confidence in Him. Then they feel relieved, as if assured that the soul they were praying for will be saved. The burden is gone, and God seems to kindly soothe the mind with a sweet assurance that the blessing will be granted.

Often, after a Christian has had this struggle, this agony in prayer, and has obtained relief in this way, he finds that the sweetest and most heavenly affections flow out. His soul rests sweetly and gloriously in God and rejoices *"with joy unspeakable and full of glory"* (1 Peter 1:8 KJV).

BINDING PRAYER

This travailing in prayer for souls also creates a remarkable bond between warmhearted Christians and young converts. Those who are converted are very dear to those who have had this spirit of prayer for them. The feeling is like that of a mother for her firstborn child. Paul expressed it beautifully when he said, *"My little children, for whom I labor in birth again until Christ is formed in you"* (Galatians 4:19). They had backslidden, and he suffered all the agonies of a parent over a wandering child. In revival, I have often noticed how those who had the spirit of prayer loved the young converts. To those who have never felt this love, what I have described does not make sense.

A CONVERSION _____

_____

_____

_____

_____

_____

PROTECTING PRAYER

Another reason God requires this sort of prayer is that it is the only way in which the church can be properly prepared to receive great blessings without being injured by them. When the church is thus prostrated in the dust before God, and is in the depths of agony in prayer, the blessing does it good. However, if the church receives the blessing without this deep humility of soul, it grows puffed up with pride. But if it is in the proper attitude, it increases in holiness, love, and humility.

INTENSE, PREVAILING PRAYER

A minister once related a story to me about a town that had not had a revival in many years. The church was nearly extinct, the youth were all unconverted, and desolation reigned unbroken. There lived, in a secluded part of the town, an aged blacksmith who stammered so badly that it was painful to hear him speak. One Friday, as he worked in his shop, alone, he became very upset about the state of the church and of the impenitent. His agony became so great that he had to put away his work, lock the shop door, and spend the afternoon in prayer.

He continued to pray all day. Then he asked his minister to arrange a conference meeting. After some hesitation, the minister consented, even though he feared few people would attend. He called the meeting for the same evening at a large private house. When evening came, more people assembled than could be accommodated in the house. All were silent for a time, until one sinner broke out in tears and said, "If anyone can pray, will he pray for me?" Another followed, and another, and still another, until people from every part of town were under deep conviction. It was also remarkable that they all dated their conviction to the hour the old man prayed in his shop. A powerful revival followed. Thus, this stammering old man's prayers prevailed, and as a prince, he had power with God. (See Genesis 32:28 KJV.)

REFLECTION ON...

PREVAILING PRAYER

_____

_____

_____

_____

_____

THE PRAYER OF FAITH

Therefore I say to you,
whatever things you ask when you pray,
believe that you receive them, and you will have them.
—Mark 11:24

There are general promises and principles laid down in the Bible that Christians would have the opportunity to use, if they would only think. Whenever you are in circumstances to which the promises or principles apply, you are to use them.

A parent can find this promise:

The mercy of the LORD is from everlasting to everlasting on those who fear Him, and His righteousness to children's children, to such as keep His covenant, and to those who remember His commandments to do them.

(Psalm 103:17–18)

This is a promise made to those who possess a certain character. If any parent knows he has this character, he can justifiably apply this promise to himself and his family. If you have this character, you are bound to make use of this promise in prayer and to believe it even for your children's children.

WHEN TO PRAY IN FAITH

Where there is any prophetic declaration that something prayed for is agreeable to the will of God, when it is plain from prophecy that the event is certainly to come, you are bound to believe it and to make it the basis of your special faith in prayer. If the time is not specified in the Bible and there is no indication of time from other sources, you are not bound to believe that it will take place in the near future. But if the time is specified, if it can be learned from studying the prophecies, and if it appears to have arrived, then Christians must understand and apply it by offering the prayer of faith.

For instance, take the case of Daniel and the return of the Jews from captivity. What did Daniel say? *"I, Daniel, understood by the books the number of the years specified by the word of the* LORD *through Jeremiah the prophet, that He would accomplish seventy years in the desolations of Jerusalem"* (Daniel 9:2). He studied his Bible and understood that the length of the captivity was to be seventy years.

What did he do then? Did he sit down on the promise and say, "God has pledged Himself to put an end to the captivity in seventy years; the time has expired, and there is no need to do anything"? Oh, no. He said, *"Then I set my face toward the Lord God to make request by prayer and supplications, with fasting, sackcloth, and ashes"* (Daniel 9:3). He set himself at once to pray that the end of the captivity would come to pass. He prayed in faith.

But what was he to believe? He believed what he learned from the prophecy. There are many prophecies yet unfulfilled in the Bible that Christians should try to understand as far as they are capable. They are then to make the prophecies the basis of believing prayer. Do not think, as some seem to, that because something is foretold in prophecy, that it is not necessary to pray for it, or that it will come whether Christians pray for it or not. God says, in regard to as yet unfulfilled events that are revealed in prophecy, *"I will also let the house of Israel inquire of Me to do this for them"* (Ezekiel 36:37).

A BIBLICAL PROPHECY

TRUSTING THE SPIRIT'S LEADING

When the Spirit of God is upon You and excites strong desires for any blessing, you are bound to pray for it in faith. You are bound to infer, from the fact that you find yourself drawn to desire such a thing while experiencing the joy and holiness the Spirit of God produces, that these desires are the work of the Spirit. People are not likely to desire with the right kind of desires unless they are inspired by the Spirit of God. The apostle referred to these desires, excited by the Spirit, in his epistle to the Romans, where he said, *"Likewise the Spirit also helps in our weaknesses. For we do not know what we should pray for as we ought, but the Spirit Himself makes intercession for us with groanings which cannot be uttered"* (Romans 8:26).

It is clear that the prayer of faith will obtain the blessing because our faith rests on evidence that it is the will of God to grant the thing. The Scripture is not evidence that something else will be granted, but that this particular thing will be.

THE FRUIT OF FAITHFUL PRAYER

People often receive more than they pray for. Solomon prayed for wisdom, and God granted him riches and honor in addition. Similarly, a wife may pray for the conversion of her husband, and if she offers the prayer in faith, God may not only grant that blessing, but also convert her child and her whole family. (See Acts 16:31.) Blessings sometimes seem to "hang together," so that if a Christian gains one, he gains them all.

I could name many individuals who decided to examine the Bible on this subject, and who, before they were through with it, were filled with the spirit of prayer. They found that God meant just what a plain, commonsense man would understand Him to mean. I advise you to try it. You have Bibles. Look them over; and whenever you find a promise you can use, plant it in your mind before you go on. You will not get through the Book without finding out that God's promises mean just what they say.

GIVING UP TOO SOON

You must persevere. You are not to pray for a thing once, then cease, and call that the prayer of faith. Look at Daniel. He prayed for twenty-one days and did not stop until he obtained the blessing. He set his heart and face toward the Lord to seek His answer by prayer and supplication. He held on for three weeks, and then the answer came. And why did it not come before? God sent an archangel with the message, but the devil hindered him. (See Daniel 10:10–14.) See what Christ said in the parable of the unjust judge and the parable of the loaves. What did He teach us by them? He taught that God will grant answers to prayer when prayer is persistent. *"Shall God not avenge His own elect who cry out day and night to Him?"* (Luke 18:7).

PERSEVERANCE_____

_____

_____

_____

_____

_____

A PREVAILING PRINCE OF PRAYER

Once a good man said to me, "Oh, I am dying of a lack of strength to pray! My body is crushed; the world is on me; how can I continue praying?" I have known that man to go to bed absolutely sick because of weakness and faintness under the pressure. And I have known him to pray as if he would do violence to heaven, and then I have seen the blessing come as plainly in answer to his prayer as if it were revealed. No person would doubt it any more than if God spoke from heaven.

This is how he died. He prayed more and more. He used to take the map of the world, look over the different countries, and pray for them until he collapsed in his room. Blessed man! He was the reproach of the ungodly and of carnal Christians. But he was the favorite of heaven and a prevailing prince in prayer.

"But," you ask, "for whom are we to pray this prayer? We want to know which cases, which people, which places, and at what times we are to pray the prayer of faith." I answer, as I have already answered, "When you have evidence—from providences, promises, prophecies, or the leadings of the Spirit—that God will do the things for which you pray."

GOD'S PROMISE TO PARENTS

You may also ask, "Did you not say there is a promise that Christian parents may apply to their children? Why is it, then, that so many faithful parents have had impenitent children who died in their sins?" This is often the case, but it proves a point, especially in view of Romans 3:4: *"Let God be true but every man a liar."* Will we believe that God has not kept His promise or that these parents did not do their duty? Perhaps they did not believe the promise or did not believe there was any such thing as the prayer of faith. Wherever you find a Christian who does not believe in any such prayer, you find in general that he has children yet in their sins.

"But," you ask, "will these views lead to fanaticism? Will people think they are offering the prayer of faith when they are not?" This is an argument against all spiritual religion whatsoever. Some people think they have it when they do not, and they are fanatics. But there are those who know what the prayer of faith is, just as there are those who know what spiritual experience is, though such prayer may be a stumbling block to coldhearted believers who do not know it. Even ministers often leave themselves open to the rebuke that Christ gave to Nicodemus: *"Are you the teacher of Israel, and do not know these things?"* (John 3:10).

GOD'S PROMISES _____

_____

_____

_____

_____

_____

UNDERSTANDING THE PRAYER OF FAITH

People who have not known by experience what the prayer of faith is have good reason to doubt their own piety. This statement is by no means unkind. Let them examine themselves. It is likely that they understand prayer as little as Nicodemus understood the new birth. (See John 3:1–9.) They have not walked with God. You cannot accurately describe the walk to them any more than you can describe a beautiful painting to a blind man.

There is reason to believe that millions are in hell because Christians have not offered the prayer of faith on their behalf. In some instances, when believers had promises under their noses, they did not have enough faith to use them. The signs of the times and the indications of providence were favorable, perhaps, and the Spirit of God prompted desires for the salvation of souls. There was evidence enough that God was ready to grant a blessing, and if Christians had only prayed in faith, God would have granted it. But He turned it away because they would not discern the signs of the times.

WHEN TO EXPECT AN ANSWER

I knew a father who was a good man, but who had misconceptions about the prayer of faith. His whole family of children were grown up, without one of them being converted. One day his son grew ill and seemed ready to die. The father prayed, but the son grew worse and was sinking into the grave without hope. The father prayed until his anguish was unutterable. Finally, when there seemed no prospect of his son surviving, he poured out his soul to God as if he would not be denied.

Later, he got an assurance that his son would not only live, but also be converted. In addition, God assured him that not only this one, but also his whole family would be converted to God. He came into the house and told his family that his son would not die. They were astonished at him. "I tell you," he said, "he will not die. And no child of mine will ever die in his sins." That man's children were all converted years ago.

What do you think of that? Was that fanaticism? If you believe it was, it is because you know nothing about the prayer of faith. Do you pray like this man prayed? Do you live in such a manner that you can offer such prayers for your children? I know that children of Christians may sometimes be converted in answer to the prayers of someone else. But do you dare leave your children to the prayers of others, when God calls you to sustain this important duty to your children?

BELIEVING THE GOOD BOOK

In conclusion, think about the efforts people are making to dispose of the Bible completely. The unsaved are in favor of doing away with the warnings of the Bible, and the church wants to do away with its promises. What does that leave? Without these, the

Bible would be an empty book. I ask in love, What is our Bible good for if we do not take hold of its precious promises and use them as the ground of our faith when we pray for the blessing of God? You would do better to send your Bibles to the non-Christians where they will do some good if you are not going to believe and use them.

THE PRAYER OF FAITH

PRAYER MEETINGS

*And whatever you ask in My name, that I will do, that the
Father may be glorified in the Son. If you ask anything in
My name, I will do it.*
—John 14:13–14

God, in His infinite grace, has created us to be sympathetic beings. Because of our nature, we communicate our feelings to one another. A minister, for instance, will often transmit his own feelings to his congregation. The Spirit of God that inspires his soul makes use of his feelings to influence his hearers just as God makes use of the words he preaches.

Nothing is more calculated to inspire a spirit of prayer than uniting in social prayer with one who has the Spirit himself, unless this one is so far ahead that his prayer will repel the rest. If others are anywhere near the level of his experience, his spirit will kindle, burn, and spread all around. One individual who obtains the spirit of prayer will often arouse a whole church, so that a general revival follows.

A PRAYER MEETING BELONGS TO THE SPIRIT

Prayer meetings ought to be given to the Spirit of God. Those who desire to pray, let them pray. If the leader sees anything that needs to be set right, let him remark freely and kindly, put it right, then go on again. He should, however, be careful to time his remarks so as not to interrupt the flow of feeling, chill the meeting, or turn the thoughts of the people from the proper subject.

Very often, those who pray long prayers in a meeting do so because they do not have the spirit of prayer. Some men will spin out a long prayer telling God who and what He is, or they will pray out a whole system of theology. Some preach, others exhort, until everybody wishes they would stop. Each one should keep to the point and pray for what he came to pray for, not follow the flights of his imagination.

THINGS THAT MAY DEFEAT A
PRAYER MEETING

Lack of Confidence in the Leader

When there is an unhappy lack of confidence in the leader, there is no hope of any good. Whatever the cause, whether he is to blame or not, the very fact that he is leading the meeting will dampen it and prevent all good. I have witnessed this in churches where there was an offensive elder or deacon (perhaps rightly judged offensive, perhaps not) placed in a leadership position, and the prayer meeting died under his influence. If there is little confidence regarding his piety, his ability, his judgment, or anything connected with the meeting, everything he says or does will fail. The same thing often takes place where the church has lost confidence in the minister.

Latecomers to the Meeting

This is a very great hindrance. After people have started praying, having their souls quiet, their eyes shut, and their attention focused on the Lord, another person bolting into the meeting will disrupt the atmosphere. Some will look up, yet all have their minds interrupted for the moment. Then everyone settles down again, and another comes in, and so on.

I suppose the devil would not care how many Christians went to a prayer meeting, if they would only arrive after the meeting had started. He would be glad to have so many go scattering along this way, dodging in very distractingly.

<small>REFLECTION ON...</small>

INTERRUPTIONS _____

_____

_____

_____

_____

_____

Too Much Singing

A great deal of singing often injures a prayer meeting. The agonizing spirit of prayer does not lead people to sing. There is a time for everything, a time to sing and a time to pray. But knowing what it is to labor in birth for souls, a Christian would never feel less like singing than when he had the spirit of prayer for sinners.

Often, a prayer meeting is injured when young converts are called on to sing joyful hymns. This is highly improper in a prayer meeting. It is not the time to let feeling flow away in joyful singing when so many sinners, even former companions, are going to hell.

Therefore, a revival is often stifled when a minister and congregation sing with young converts at the meeting. When they rejoice while they should be feeling more and more deeply for sinners, they grieve away the Spirit of God, and they soon find that their agony and travail of soul are gone.

Long Meetings

Prayer meetings are often too long. People in attendance should always be dismissed while there is still fervency. Meetings should not drag out until all feeling is exhausted and the spirit of prayer is gone.

Meeting Leader's Lack of Preparation

Every minister should know that if prayer meetings are neglected, all his work is in vain. Unless he can convince Christians to attend the prayer meetings, nothing else he can do will improve the state of faith.

Prayer meetings are the most difficult meetings to sustain—as, indeed, they ought to be. They are so spiritual that unless the leader is especially prepared, both in heart and mind, they will dwindle. It is useless for the leader to complain if members of the church do not attend.

In nine cases out of ten, it is the leader's fault that people do not attend. If he showed interest in the meeting and its purpose, those who attended would find the meeting so interesting they would attend regularly. If he is so cold, dull, and lacking in spirituality as to freeze everything, it would be no wonder if people did not come to the meeting.

Church officers often complain and scold because people do not come to the prayer meeting, when the truth is, they themselves are so cold that they spiritually and emotionally freeze to death everyone who does come.

The great objective of all the means of grace is to aim directly at the conversion of sinners. You should pray that they will be converted there. Do not pray that they will merely be awakened and convicted, but pray that they may be converted on the spot. No one should pray or make any remarks as if he expected a single sinner would go away without giving his heart to God. You should all make the impression on the sinner's mind that now is the time to give his life to Jesus. If you do this while you are still speaking, God will hear.

Today, not tomorrow; not next
Week but To day!!

PRAYER MEETINGS _____

_____

_____

_____

_____

_____

HINDRANCES TO REVIVALS

So I sent messengers to them, saying, "I am doing a great work, so that I cannot come down. Why should the work cease while I leave it and go down to you?"
—Nehemiah 6:3

When Christians become proud of their "great revival," it will stop. I mean those Christians who have been instrumental in promoting it.

It is almost always the case with a revival that a part of the church proves too proud or too worldly to take any part in the work. They are determined to stand aloof and to wait and see what its outcome will be. However, the pride of this part of the church cannot stop the revival, because the revival never depended on them. It began without them, and it can go on without them. They may fold their arms and do nothing but watch and find fault, yet the work will go on.

THINGS THAT HINDER REVIVAL

Pride

But when the part of the church that does the work begins to think what a great revival they have had, how they have labored and prayed, how bold and how zealous they have been, and how much good they have done, the work is likely to decline.

For example, perhaps the newspapers have published what a revival there has been in that church and how absorbed the members have been. They begin to think how high they will stand in the estimation of other churches all over the land because they have had such a great revival. And so they get puffed up and vain, and they can no longer enjoy the presence of God. The Spirit withdraws from them, and the revival ceases.

Again, the Spirit may be grieved by a spirit of boasting about the revival. Sometimes, as soon as a revival starts, you will see it advertised in the newspapers. Usually this will kill the revival. There was such a case in a neighboring state where a revival had started. The pastor immediately published a letter saying that he was holding a revival. I saw the letter and said to myself, "That is the last we will hear of this revival."

And so it was. In a few days, the work ceased. I could mention other cases and places where people published such things and the church became puffed up and the people became so proud that little more could be done for the revival.

Also, when Christians begin to proselytize, revival stops. Perhaps a revival will go on for a time, and all sectarian difficulties are forgotten until somebody circulates a book, privately, to gain new converts for selfish purposes. Perhaps some overzealous deacon, some mischief-making woman, or some proselytizing minister cannot keep quiet any longer but begins to do the work of the devil by attempting to gain new converts. By doing this, he or she stirs up bitterness, raises a selfish strife, grieves away the Spirit, and drives Christians into factions. No more revival there!

CHURCH PRIDE _____

_____

_____

_____

_____

_____

Exalting Self over God

Some people, under the pretense of publishing things to the praise and glory of God, have in fact published things that seemed to exalt themselves more. They seemed to be making their own participation conspicuous. At a long series of meetings held in a church some time ago, there were five hundred individuals hopefully converted. We knew their names and addresses as well. A considerable number of them joined this church. Many of them united with other churches.

Nothing was mentioned, however, in the papers. I have been asked several times why we were so silent about the revival. I could only reply that there was such a tendency to self-exaltation in the churches that I was afraid to publish anything on the subject. Perhaps I made a mistake. But I have so often seen mischief done by premature publications that I thought it would be best to say nothing about it.

EXALTING SELF _____

_____

_____

_____

_____

_____

Prejudice and Lack of Love

A revival is likely to stop when Christians lose the spirit of brotherly love. Jesus Christ will not continue with people in a revival any longer than they continue in the exercise of brotherly love. When Christians are in the spirit of a revival, they feel this love. Then you will hear them call each other "Brother" and "Sister" very affectionately.

But when they begin to get cold, they lose this affection for one another, and then using "Brother" and "Sister" seems silly. So they stop using it. In some churches, they never use these names, but where there is revival, Christians naturally use them.

I never saw a revival, and probably there never was one, in which they did not do this. But as soon as the spirit of love begins to cease, the Spirit of God becomes so grieved that He leaves.

Christians of all denominations should forget their prejudices. Vast multitudes of believers have indulged prejudice to such a degree as to be unwilling to read, hear, or come to a right understanding on the subject. Christians cannot pray in this state of mind. I deny that anyone possesses the spirit of prayer while he is too prejudiced to examine this or any other question of duty.

If the light did not shine, Christians could remain in the dark on this point and still possess the spirit of prayer. But if they refuse to come to the light, they cannot pray. Where ministers, individual Christians, or whole churches resist the truth on this point, I do not believe they will or can enjoy a revival.

PREJUDICE _____

_____

_____

_____

_____

_____

Inconsistent Ministering

Ordinarily, a lengthy series of meetings should be conducted throughout by the same minister, if possible. Sometimes, through courtesy, visiting ministers are asked to speak. Unfortunately, this does not bring blessing. The reason is obvious. They did not come in a state of mind that was right for entering into this work, and they did not know the state of the congregation's mind so as to know what to preach.

Suppose a person who is sick would call a different physician every day. None of the physicians would know what the symptoms had been, what was the course of the disease or treatment, what remedies had been tried, or what the patient could bear. This method would certainly kill the patient.

In a similar way, a long series of meetings carried on by a succession of ministers could be harmful. None of the ministers will get into the spirit of it, and, generally, they will do more harm than good.

A meeting should not, ordinarily, be arranged unless the right kind of help can be secured and a minister or two can be obtained who will agree to stay until the meeting is finished. Then the church will probably secure a rich blessing.

Not Preaching for the Times

It is evident that we must have more stirring preaching to meet our needs today. Ministers are generally beginning to find this out. Some of them complain and assume it to be owing to "new measures," as they call them. They think that new measures have perverted the taste of the people. But this is not the problem. The character of the age has changed, but these men retain the same commonplace style of preaching that was effective half a century ago.

Look at the early Methodists. Many of their ministers were taken right from the shop or farm, and yet they gathered congregations and won souls everywhere. Wherever they went, their plain, pointed, and simple but warm and animated mode of preaching always gathered congregations. We must have powerful preaching! Even a preacher without an extensive education will draw a congregation around him when he has an earnest style and pours out fire on his hearers when he preaches.

RELEVANCE _____

_____

_____

_____

_____

_____

Merely Going Through the Motions

Other things may stop a revival. Some people talk very foolishly on this subject, as if nothing could hinder a genuine revival. They say, "If your revival is a work of God, it cannot be stopped. Can any created being stop God?" Now, I ask, is this common sense?

Formerly, it used to be the established belief that a revival could not be stopped because it was the work of God. And so everyone assumed it would go on, no matter what might be done to hinder it, in the church or out of it. The farmer might just as well reason that he could go, cut down his wheat, and not hurt the crop, because God makes grain grow.

A revival is the work of God, and so is a crop of wheat. God is as much dependent on the use of means in one case as the other. Therefore, a revival is as liable to be injured as a wheat field.

A revival will cease when Christians become mechanical in their attempts to promote it. When their faith is strong, their hearts fervent and ripe, their prayers full of holy emotion, and their words full of power, the work goes on. But when their prayers begin to be cold and without emotion, when they begin to labor mechanically and to use words without feelings, then the revival will cease.

The revival will stop when the church grows exhausted through its labor. Multitudes of Christians make a great mistake here in times of revival. They are so thoughtless and have so little judgment that they will break up all their habits of living, neglect to eat and sleep at the proper hours, and let the excitement run away with them. By doing this, they overwork their bodies and soon become exhausted. It then becomes impossible for them to continue in the work. Revivals often cease because of negligence and imprudence in this area on the part of those in charge of the revival.

Stealing God's Laurels

Whenever Christians do not feel their dependence on the Spirit, whenever Christians believe they are strong in their own strength, God curses their blessings. In many instances, they sin against their own mercies because they become proud of their success, take the credit themselves, and do not give the glory to God. As He says,

> *"If you will not hear, and if you will not take it to heart, to give glory to My name," says the LORD of hosts, "I will send a curse upon you, and I will curse your blessings. Yes, I have cursed them already, because you do not take it to heart."*
>
> (Malachi 2:2)

There has been a great deal of this, undoubtedly. I have seen many things in the newspaper that suggested man's tendency to take credit for success in promoting revivals. This is no doubt a great temptation, and it requires the utmost watchfulness on the part of ministers and churches so that conceited men do not grieve the Spirit.

Not Having Ongoing Revival

A revival will decline and cease unless Christians are frequently revived. By this I mean that Christians, in order to keep in the spirit of revival, need to be frequently convicted and humbled before God. The idea of a Christian being revived is something that many do not understand. But the fact is that, even during a revival, the Christian's heart is able to get crusted over and lose its exquisite desire for divine things. His anointing and prevalence in prayer abate, and he must be renewed again.

It is impossible to keep a Christian in such a holy state unless he passes through such a process every few days. I have never worked revivals with anyone who wanted to continue the work and be fit to manage a revival who did not pass through this process of repentance every two or three weeks.

REFLECTION ON...

ONGOING REVIVAL _____

_____

_____

_____

_____

_____

Conflict within the Ranks

Revival can be put down by the continued opposition of the old school combined with a bad spirit in the new school. If those who do nothing to promote revival continue their opposition, and if those who are working to promote it allow themselves to grow impatient and develop a bad spirit, the revival will cease. When the old school writes letters in the papers against revival or revivalists, and the new school answers in a contentious spirit, revival will cease.

Let them keep to their work and neither talk about the opposition nor preach on it, nor rush into print about it. If others choose to publish slander, let the Lord's people keep to their work. None of the slander will stop the revival while those who are engaged in it mind their own business and keep to their work.

INTERNAL CONFLICT _____

_____

_____

_____

_____

_____

Neglecting Missions

Another thing that hinders revival is neglecting the claims of missions. If Christians confine their attention to their own church, do not even read their missionary magazines, do not inform themselves about missions, and do not do what God calls them to do, the Spirit of God will depart from them.

Not Sanctifying the Sabbath

If the church wishes to promote revival, it must sanctify the Sabbath. There is a great deal of Sabbath-breaking in the land. Merchants break it, travelers break it, and the government breaks it.

One thing is most certain: unless something is done quickly and effectively to promote the sanctification of the Sabbath by the church, it will no longer be a special day. And what can the church do, what will this nation do, without any Sabbath?

HINDRANCES TO REVIVAL _____

_____

_____

_____

_____

_____

WINNING SOULS
REQUIRES WISDOM

He who wins souls is wise.
—Proverbs 11:30

There are many things to remember when dealing with a careless sinner. Timing is important. You must select a proper time to try to make a serious impression on the mind of a careless sinner. If you fail to select the most proper time, you will most likely be defeated.

USE THE RIGHT TIMING

It is desirable, if possible, to address a person who is careless, when he is away from other activities. It is important to talk with a person when he is not excited about any other subject. Otherwise, he will not be in the right frame of mind to discuss Christianity.

Be sure that the person is completely sober. Otherwise, he is unfit to be approached on the subject of Christianity. If he has been drinking, you know there is little chance of producing any lasting effect on him.

If possible, when you wish to discuss salvation, talk to a man when he is in a good mood. If you find him in a bad mood, he will probably become angry and abuse you. It is better to leave him alone for that time.

If possible, always take the opportunity to converse with careless sinners when they are alone. Most men are too proud to discuss themselves freely in the presence of others, even their own families.

In visiting families, instead of calling the entire family together at the same time, it is better to see each member, one at a time.

For example, there was a Christian woman who kept a boardinghouse for young gentlemen. She had twenty-one of them in her house, and she eventually became anxious for their salvation. She made it the subject of prayer, but saw no seriousness among them. At length, she saw that something must be done in addition to praying, yet she did not know what.

One morning, after breakfast, as the rest were leaving, she asked one of them to stop a few minutes. She took him aside and tenderly discussed Christ with him and prayed with him. She followed up the impression made, and he was soon converted.

Then she spoke to another, and so on, taking one at a time. She never let the rest know what was going on, so as not to alarm them, until all these young men were converted. Now, if she had brought the subject before all of them together, very likely, they would have ridiculed the idea. Or perhaps they would have been offended and left the house, and she could have had no further influence over them. But by taking each one alone and treating him respectfully and kindly, he had no motive for resistance, as often arises when one is in the presence of others.

WITNESSING

SPEAK WITH SERIOUSNESS

Be serious! Avoid all lightness of manner or language. Levity will produce anything but a right impression. You ought to feel that you are engaged in very serious work that is going to affect the character of your friend or neighbor and probably determine his destiny for eternity. Who could trifle and use levity in such circumstances if his heart were sincere?

SPEAK WITH RESPECT

Be respectful. Some think it is necessary to be abrupt, rude, and coarse in their discussions with the careless and impenitent. No mistake can be greater. The apostle Peter gave us a better rule on the subject, when he said, *"Be tenderhearted, be courteous; not returning evil for evil or reviling for reviling, but on the contrary blessing"* (1 Peter 3:8–9).

USE FUNDAMENTAL TRUTHS

Bring the great and fundamental truths to bear on the person's mind. Sinners are very likely to run off on some tangent, or some secondary point, especially one where there is a denominational difference.

Tell him the purpose is to save his soul and not settle controversial questions in theology. Hold him to the great fundamental points by which he can choose to be saved or lost.

BE SPECIFIC

Bring up the individual's particular sins. Talking in general terms against sin will produce no results. You must make a man feel that you mean *him*. A minister who cannot make his hearers feel that he means them cannot expect to accomplish much. Some people are very careful to avoid mentioning the particular sins of which they know the individual to be guilty, for fear of hurting his feelings. This is wrong. If you know his history, bring up his particular sins. Kindly, but plainly, not being offensive, awaken his conscience and give full force to the truth.

BE BRIEF

It is generally best to be brief and not long-winded about what you have to say. Bring his attention, as soon as you can, to the point. Say a few things, press them home, and bring the matter to a conclusion. If possible, get the individual to repent and give himself to Christ at the time. This is the proper conclusion. Carefully avoid making an impression that you do not wish him to repent *now*.

BE PERSISTENT

Whenever you have reason to believe that a person within your reach is awakened, do not sleep until you have poured the light into his mind and have tried to bring him to immediate repentance. Then be persistent in your attempts to persuade the individual to accept Jesus as his Savior.

Sometimes there is a particular sin that he will not forsake. He pretends it is only a small one or tries to persuade himself it is no sin at all. No matter how small it is, he can never get into the kingdom of God until he gives it up. God knows nothing about "small" sins.

WITNESSING

PUT THE FOCUS ON CHRIST

Sometimes people will strenuously maintain that they have committed the unpardonable sin. When they get this idea into their minds, they will turn everything you say against themselves. In some cases, it is good to take them on their own ground and reason with them in this way: "Suppose you have committed the unpardonable sin; what then? It is reasonable that you submit to God, be sorry for your sins, and break off from them. Do all the good you can, even if God will not forgive you. Even if you go to hell, you ought to do this." Be persistent with this thought until you find they understand and consent to it.

It is common for people like this to keep their eyes on themselves. They will shut themselves up, looking at their own darkness instead of looking to Christ. Now, if you can take their minds off themselves and get them to think of Christ, you can draw them away from brooding over their own present feelings. Then they can grasp the hope set before them in the gospel.

STRESS ENTIRE CONSECRATION

The church is filled with hypocrites because people were never made to see that they must make an entire consecration of everything to Christ. All their time, all their talents, and all their influence must be surrendered to God or they will never get to heaven. Many think they can be Christians, yet they dream through life, using all their time and property for themselves. They will give a little now and then, when they can give with perfect convenience. This is a sad mistake, and they will find this to be true if they do not employ their energies for God. When they die, instead of finding heaven at the end of the path they are pursuing, they will find hell.

WAKE UP THE CHURCH FIRST

Here is a point where almost all ministers fail. They do not know how to wake up the church. They cannot raise a high standard of piety and clear the way for the works of conversion. Many ministers can preach to sinners very well. But because of the counteracting influence of the sinful church body, they have difficulty maintaining their converts. Very often, they also find it difficult to remove the sin and coldness within their congregations. There are only a few ministers in the country who know how to probe the church when it is in a cold, backslidden state. They can effectively awaken the members and keep them awake.

When the members of the church become very cold, it is extremely difficult to stir them up. They have a form of piety that wards off the truth. At the same time, it is just this kind of piety that has no power or efficiency and repels new believers. Such Christians are the most difficult individuals to arouse from their slumber. I do not mean that they are always more wicked than the impenitent. These individuals are often constructively involved in their churches, and pass for very good Christians, but they are useless in a revival.

A PRAYER FOR...

Your church _____

_____

_____

_____

_____

_____

ADAPT SERMONS TO PARTICULAR GROUPS

To reach different classes of sinners successfully requires great wisdom on the part of a minister. For instance, a sermon on a particular subject may impress a particular group among his hearers. Perhaps they will begin to look serious, talk about it, or split hairs about it. Now, if the minister is wise, he will know how to observe these indications, and follow them up with sermons adapted to this group until he leads them into the kingdom of God.

When this group is saved, it is time to find out where another group is hiding, break down their refuges, and follow them until they come into the kingdom. He should thus search for every place where sinners hide, just as the voice of God followed Adam in the garden, "[Adam,] *where are you?*" (Genesis 3:9), until one group of hearers after another is brought in. In this way, the whole community will be converted.

A minister must be very wise to do this.

The best educated ministers are those who win the most souls. Some ministers are looked down on and accused of being ignorant because they do not have a formal education, although they are very far from being ignorant of the great thing for which the ministry is appointed. This is wrong! Learning is important and always useful. But, after all, a minister may know how to win souls to Christ without a formal education. The minister who can win the most souls to Christ can give the best education to another minister or seminary student.

PREPARE YOUNG MINISTERS
FOR REVIVAL

When young ministers come out of the seminaries, are they prepared to go into a revival? Notice the churches where a revival is in progress and where they are in need of a minister. They will probably not ask for a new minister from a theological seminary. A new minister can seldom work on a revival, sustain it, and bring it to a successful conclusion. Like David with Saul's armor, he will come in with such a load of unnecessary theological doctrines that he will not know what to do. Leave him there for two weeks, and the revival will come to an end. The churches know and feel that the greater part of these young men do not know how to do anything that needs to be done for a revival. It is a sad state of things when a church could ask every seminary in the country to send a minister and only be able to find a few young preachers who could conduct a revival.

Your minister _____

_____

_____

_____

_____

_____

KEEP PROFESSORS IN TOUCH WITH THE CHURCH

It is evident to me that seminary professors should preach regularly and mingle with various churches. Otherwise, they will not understand current issues facing the church, nor will they be able to properly train young ministers. It is a shame and a sin that theological professors who seldom preach, and who are withdrawn from the active duties of the ministry, can sit in their offices and write letters of advice and instruction to ministers when they are so isolated from the field. They often cannot judge what must be done.

The men who spend all, or at least a portion, of their time in the active duties of the ministry are the only men who are able to judge what measures are prudent or imprudent. It is as dangerous and ridiculous for our theological professors who are withdrawn from the field of conflict to be allowed to dictate the measure and movements of the church as it would be for a general to sit in his home and attempt to order a battle.

IMPORTANCE OF WISDOM IN WINNING SOULS

Now, who among us can claim to possess such divine wisdom? Can you, laymen? Can you, ministers? Are we using wisdom as we try to win souls, or do we believe that success is no criterion of wisdom?

How few of you have ever had wisdom enough to convert so much as a single sinner? Do not say, "I cannot convert sinners. God alone can convert sinners." Look at the Scripture: *"He who wins souls is wise."* It is true that God converts sinners. But there is a sense, too, in which ministers convert them.

Men! Women! You must be wise in winning souls. Perhaps souls have already perished because you have not used wisdom to save them. The city is going to hell. Yes, the world is going to hell and will continue to do so until the church finds out how to win souls.

WISDOM TO WIN SOULS _____

_____

_____

_____

_____

_____

HOW TO
APPROACH SINNERS

Behold, I send you out as sheep in the midst of wolves.
Therefore be wise as serpents and harmless as doves.
—Matthew 10:16

Seize the earliest opportunity to talk with those around you who are careless. Do not put it off from day to day, thinking a better opportunity will come. You must seek an opportunity, and if you cannot find one, make one. Set a special time or place and arrange to meet with your friend or neighbor where you can speak with him freely. Send him a note or make a special trip to see him. Then he will feel that this is important to you. Follow it up until you succeed or become convinced that, for now, nothing more can be done.

BE KIND

When you approach a careless individual, be sure to treat him kindly. Let him see that you are not talking with him because you seek a quarrel with him, but because you love his soul and desire his best good in time and eternity. If you are harsh and overbearing, you will probably offend him and drive him farther away from the way of life.

BE PLAIN

Be sure to be very plain. Do not cover up any part of the person's character or his relationship to God. Lay it all open, not to offend or wound him, but because it is necessary. Before you can cure a wound, you must probe it to the bottom. Keep back none of the truth, but let it come out plainly before him.

BE PATIENT

Be very patient. If he has a real difficulty in his mind, be very patient until you find out what it is; then clear it up. If his problem is just a matter of splitting hairs, help him to see the insignificance of the issue compared with salvation. Do not try to answer with argument, but show him that he is not sincere in advancing his argument. It is not worthwhile to spend your time arguing over incidentals. Enlist his conscience on your side.

GUARD YOUR OWN SPIRIT

Be careful to guard your own spirit. There are many people who do not have the proper temperament for discussing issues with those who are very opposed to religion. Such people only want to see you become angry. They will go away very pleased with themselves because they have "made one of these saints mad."

DO NOT TAKE SIDES WITH THE SINNER AGAINST GOD

If the sinner is inclined to entrench himself against God, be careful not to take his part in anything. If he says he cannot do his duty, do not take sides with him or say anything to support his falsehood. Do not tell him he cannot do anything or help maintain the controversy against his Maker. Sometimes a careless sinner will find fault with Christians. Do not side with him against Christians. Just tell him he does not have to answer for their sins. It is better for him to pay attention to his own concerns. If you agree with him, he feels that he has you on his side. Show him that it is a wicked and critical spirit that prompts him to make these remarks, not concern for the honor of religion or the laws of Jesus Christ.

IDENTIFY IDOLS

Sometimes the individual has an idol, something that he loves more than God, which prevents him from giving himself up to Him. You must search out and see what it is that he will not give up. Perhaps it is wealth, perhaps an earthly friend, perhaps fancy clothes or the partying crowd, or some favorite amusement. At any rate, there is something on which his heart is so set that he will not yield to God.

REFLECTION ON...

Idols

RECOGNIZE BARRIERS

Sinners may have entrenched themselves somewhere and fortified their minds in regard to some particular point that they are determined not to yield. For instance, they may have decided they will not do a particular thing.

I know a man, a lawyer, who was determined not to go into a certain grove in the woods to pray. Several other people during the revival had gone into the grove in the woods, and there, by prayer and meditation, had given themselves to God. His own employee had been converted there. But the lawyer had powerful convictions and went for weeks in his determination.

He tried to make God believe that it was not pride that kept him from Christ; so he decided that, on his way home from a meeting, he would kneel down in the street and pray. He would even look for a mud puddle in the street where he could kneel to show he was not proud. He once prayed all night in his parlor—but he would not go into the grove.

Eventually, his distress became greater. He was so angry with God that he sank into a great depression. Finally, he decided to go into the woods and pray. As soon as he got there, he was converted, and he poured out his full heart to God.

LEARN HOW TO BUILD UP THE KINGDOM

Make it an object of constant study, daily reflection, and prayer to learn how to deal with sinners and to promote their conversion. It is the great commission of every Christian to save souls. People often complain that they do not know how to handle this matter. Yet these same people have never taken the time to qualify themselves for the work. If people were as careless in preparing themselves for their worldly business as they are to save souls, how do you think they would succeed?

Now, if you are neglecting the main business of life, what are you living for? If you do not take the time to find out how you can help build up the kingdom of Christ, you are not fulfilling your role as a Christian.

Anxious sinners are in a very serious and critical state. They have, in fact, come to a turning point. It is a time when their destiny is likely to be settled forever. Christians ought to feel deeply for them. In many respects, their circumstances are more serious than those of the Final Judgment. The Judgment Day reveals their destiny. But here their destiny is decided. And the particular time when it is done is when the Spirit is striving with them.

WITNESSING _____

_____

_____

_____

_____

THE NECESSITY OF UNION

Again I say to you that if two of you agree on earth
concerning anything that they ask, it will be done for them
by My Father in heaven.
—Matthew 18:19

One individual may desire a revival for the glory of God and the salvation of sinners. Another member of the church may also desire a revival, but for very different motives. Some, perhaps, desire a revival in order to have the congregation built up and strengthened. This would make it easier for them to pay their expenses in supporting the gospel.

Another desires a revival for the sake of having the church increased so as to be more respectable. Others desire a revival because they have been opposed or slandered, and they wish to have it known that, whatever may be thought or said, God blesses them. Sometimes, people desire a revival from mere natural affection, so as to have their friends converted and saved.

People can pray so emphatically for a revival that you would think by their earnestness and unity that they would certainly move God to grant the blessing, until you find out their reason. And what is it? They see their congregation is about to be broken up unless something can be done. Or they see another denomination gaining ground, and there is no way to counteract this except by having a revival in their church. All their praying is, therefore, only an attempt to get the Almighty to help them out of their difficulty. It is purely selfish and offensive to God.

AGREEING WITH GOD BRINGS REVIVAL

Many parents seldom agree in praying for the conversion of their children in such a way as to have their prayers answered until they recognize that their children are rebels. Parents often pray very earnestly for their children. But if they want their prayers to prevail, they must take God's part against their children, acknowledging that, because of their perverseness and depraved wickedness, He is obliged to send them to hell unless they are saved.

I knew a woman who was very anxious for the salvation of her son. She used to pray for him with agony, but still he remained impenitent. Finally, she became convinced that her prayers and agonies were nothing but the fond yearnings of parental love, not dictated at all by a just view of her son's character as a willful and wicked rebel against God. No impression was ever made on his mind until she took a strong stand against him as a rebel and saw that he deserved to be sent to hell. Only then was he converted. The reason was that she never before was influenced by the right motive.

HOLDING SINNERS ACCOUNTABLE

Suppose a church gets the idea that sinners are poor, unfortunate creatures who come into the world with such a nature that they cannot help sinning. If Christians feel that sinners are unable to repent and believe the gospel, it is hard for them to see the sinner as a rebel against God who deserves to be sent to hell. How can they feel the sinner is to blame? And how can they take God's part when they pray?

If they do not take God's part against the sinner, they cannot expect God to hear their prayers, because they do not pray with right motives. No doubt, one great reason so many prayers are not answered is that those who pray take the sinner's part against God. They pray as if the sinner were a poor, unfortunate being to be pitied, rather than a guilty wretch to be blamed. And the reason is that they do not believe sinners are able to obey God.

How often do you hear people pray for sinners in this style: "O Lord, help this poor soul to do what he is required to do. O Lord, enable him to do so-and-so"? Now, this language implies that they take the sinner's part and not God's. They cannot pray successfully until they understand that the sinner is an obstinate rebel. He is so obstinate that, without the Holy Spirit, he never will become converted. This obstinacy is the only reason he needs the influence of the Holy Spirit for his conversion. The sinner needs help in overcoming his obstinacy, making him willing to do what God justly requires him to do.

Taking God's part _____

_____

_____

_____

_____

REMOVING REBELLIOUS CHURCH MEMBERS

If there are rebellious and impenitent members in the church, they should be removed. The church should agree to cut them off. If they remain, they are a reproach to religion and will hinder revival. Sometimes, when an attempt is made to cast them out, there is a division. Then the work is stopped. Sometimes, the offenders are influential people, or they have family friends who will take their side, create a bad spirit, and prevent revival.

CONFESSION OF SIN

Whenever wrong has been done to anyone, there should be a full confession. I do not mean a cold and forced acknowledgment, such as saying, "If I have done wrong, I am sorry for it." It should be a hearty confession, going the full length of the wrong and showing that it comes out of a broken heart.

A PRAYER FOR...

UNITY _____

_____

_____

_____

_____

FORGIVENESS AND A CHRISTLIKE SPIRIT

A great obstruction to revival is often found where active, leading individuals harbor a revengeful and unforgiving spirit toward those who have injured them. If the church members are truly in agreement in confessing their faults and in cherishing a tender, merciful, forgiving, Christlike spirit toward anyone they think has done them wrong, the Spirit will come down upon them, overflowing their souls.

UNITY AND REVIVAL _____

_____

_____

_____

_____

_____

DIRECTIONS TO SINNERS

What must I do to be saved?
—Acts 16:30

No directions to sinners should be given that do not include a change of heart, a right heart, or vigorous obedience to Christ. In other words, nothing is proper that does not imply actually becoming a Christian. Any other direction that falls short of this is of no use. It will not bring a sinner any nearer to the kingdom, but it will lead him to put off doing the very thing that he must do in order to be saved.

A RIGHT STATE OF HEART

The sinner should be told plainly, at once, what he must do if he does not wish to be lost. He should be told nothing that does not include a right state of heart. Whatever he does that does not include a right heart is sin. Whether he reads the Bible or not, he is in sin as long as he remains in rebellion. Whether he goes to church or stays away, whether he prays or not, he is living in rebellion. It is surprising that a sinner could think he was doing God a service just by reading the Bible or attending church.

Would a rebel against the government read the law book while he continued in rebellion without the intention to obey?

Would he ask for pardon while he held on to his weapons of resistance and warfare? Would you think he was doing his country a service and feel obligated to show him favor? No. You would say that all his reading and asking for pardon were only an insult to the majesty both of the lawgiver and the law.

Likewise, sinners, while they remain in impenitence, are insulting God whether they read His Word and pray or leave these things alone. No matter what place or what position his body is in (on his knees or in the house of God), as long as his heart is not right, as long as he resists the Holy Spirit and rejects Christ, he is a rebel against his Maker.

BELIEF IN THE LORD JESUS CHRIST

It is generally safe to tell a sinner to repent. Generally. Sometimes, the Spirit of God seems not so much to direct the sinner's attention to his own sins as to some other thing. In the days of the apostles, people seem to have been agitated mainly by the question of whether Jesus was the true Messiah. The apostles therefore directed most of their instruction to proving that He was the Christ. Whenever anxious sinners asked what they had to do, the apostles usually exhorted them to *"believe on the Lord Jesus Christ"* (Acts 16:31).

They emphasized this point because this was where the Spirit of God was striving, and this was the subject that especially stirred up the minds of the people. Consequently, this probably was the first thing a person accepted when he submitted to God. The big issue in those days was whether or not the Jew and the Gentile believed that Jesus was the Son of God.

BELIEF _____

_____

_____

_____

_____

_____

TRUE REPENTANCE

At other times, the Spirit of God deals with sinners regarding their own sins. Sometimes, He deals with them in regard to a particular duty, perhaps family prayer. The sinner will often argue the point with God as to whether it is right for him to pray, or whether he ought to pray in his family. I have known striking cases where the individual was struggling on this point, and as soon as he fell to his knees to pray, he yielded his heart. This showed that the Spirit of God knew exactly where the hinge to this sinner's conversion was hidden.

Words that used to be plain and easily understood have now become so perverted that they need to be explained to sinners, or they will often convey a wrong impression to their minds. This is the case with the word *repentance*. Many suppose that remorse or a sense of guilt is repentance. Then hell is full of repentance because it is full of unutterable and eternal remorse.

Others feel regret that they have sinned, and they call that repenting. But they regret their sin only because of the consequences, not because they abhor sin. This is not repentance. Others suppose that conviction of sin and strong fears of hell are repentance. Others consider the regret of conscience as repentance. They say, "I never do anything wrong without repenting and feeling sorry I did it."

Sinners must learn that all these things are not repentance. Not only are they consistent with the utmost wickedness, but the devil could also experience them all and still remain a devil. Repentance is a change of mind toward God and sin. It is not only a change of views, but also a change of the ultimate preference or choice of the soul and of action. It is a voluntary change and, consequently, involves a change of feeling and action toward God and sin.

This is the same type of change of mind as when one changes interests. If we hear that a man has changed his mind in politics, everyone understands that he has undergone a change in his views, feelings, and conduct. This is repentance on that subject. It is a change of mind, but not toward God. Evangelical repentance is a change of will, feeling, and life in respect to God.

Repentance always implies abhorrence of sin. It involves, of course, the love of God and the forsaking of sin. The sinner who truly repents does not feel the way sinners think they would feel when giving up their sins. Impenitent sinners see religion in this way: they think that if they become Christian, they would have to stay away from pornography, drunkenness, gambling, or other things they now enjoy. They think they could never enjoy themselves if they stopped doing all those things.

This is far from the truth. Christianity does not make the believer unhappy by keeping him away from the sinful things he loved, because the believer has changed his opinion of those things. The unsaved do not seem to realize that the person who has repented has no desire for these things. He has given them up and turned his mind away from them. Sinners feel that giving these things up would be a continual sacrifice that would always make them unhappy. This is a great mistake.

I know there are some Christians who would be very glad to return to their former practices. However, they feel constrained by the fear of losing their reputation. They can feel this way because they have not completely repented of their sins, or perhaps they do not even hate sin. Repentance always consists of a change of views and feelings

If a person was truly converted, instead of choosing these things, he would turn away from them with loathing. Instead of lusting after the luxuries of Egypt and desiring to go into their former circles, parties, and the like, they would find their highest pleasure in obeying God.

REFLECTION ON...

Repentance _____

_____

_____

_____

_____

_____

CONFESSING AND FORSAKING SIN

Another must for sinners is to confess and forsake their sins. They must confess to God their sins against God and confess to men their sins against men. Forsake them all. A man has not forsaken his sins until he has made as much reparation for them as is in his power.

If he has stolen money or defrauded his neighbor of property, he does not forsake his sins by merely resolving not to steal anymore or to cheat again; he must make restitution to the extent of his power.

If he has slandered anyone, he does not forsake his sin by merely saying he will not do so again; he must make reparation. In like manner, if he has robbed God, as all sinners have, he must make restitution as much as he can.

Suppose a man made money while living in rebellion against God. He withheld his time, talents, and service from God, lived and indulged in the bounties of God's providence, and refused to give to the work of the salvation of the world. He has robbed God. If he were to die thinking the money was only his, and were to leave his total fortune to his heirs, without consulting the will of God, he would certainly be condemned to hell as a robber.

He has never made any satisfaction to God. With all his whining and pious talk, he has never confessed his sin to God, forsaken his sin, or acknowledged himself as God's steward. If he refuses to hold the property in his possession as the steward of God, and instead considers it as his own, and as such gives it to his children, he says to God, in effect, "That property is not Yours; it is mine, and I will give it to my children." He has continued in his sin because he does not relinquish the ownership of what he has stolen from God.

What would a merchant think if his clerk took the capital, set up a store of his own, and died with it in his hands? Would this man go to heaven? "No," you say. "God would prove Himself unjust to let such a character go unpunished." What, then, do we say of the man who has robbed God all of his life?

God sent this man to be His clerk and to manage some of His affairs. But this man has stolen all the money, claiming it as his. At his death, he left it to his children, as if it were all his own lawful property. Has that man forsaken sin? No! If he has not surrendered himself and all he has to God, he has not even taken the first step on the way to heaven.

CONFESSION _____

_____

_____

_____

_____

_____

WILLING RIGHT

Sometimes sinners imagine they must wait for different feelings before they submit to God. They say, "I do not think I feel right enough yet to accept Christ." They need to be told that God requires them to will right. If they obey and submit with the will, the feelings will adjust themselves in due time. It is not a question of feeling, but of willing and acting.

Feelings are involuntary and have no moral character except what they derive from the action of the will, with which action they sympathize. Therefore, correct feelings only follow correction in the will.

The sinner should come to Christ by accepting Him immediately. He must not do this in obedience to his feelings, but in obedience to his conscience. Obey, submit, trust. Give up everything to God instantly, and your feelings will follow correctly. Do not wait for better feelings, but commit your whole being to God at once. This will soon result in the feelings for which you are waiting. God requires the present act of your mind, turning from sin to holiness, and from the service of Satan to the service of the living God.

A PRAYER FOR...

DIRECTING PEOPLE TO CHRIST _____

_____

_____

_____

_____

_____

FALSE COMFORTS FOR SINNERS

How then can you comfort me with empty words,
since falsehood remains in your answers?
—Job 21:34

No doubt, millions and millions are now in hell because those around them gave them false comfort. These "friends" were full of false pity or so much in the dark themselves that they did not let sinners remain anxious until they submitted their hearts to God.

THE NECESSITY OF SEEING
ONE'S SINS FOR WHAT THEY ARE

I have often had Christians bring anxious sinners to me and beg me to comfort them. When I have probed the conscience of the sinner to the quick, the believers have shuddered and sometimes taken the sinner's side. It is sometimes impossible to deal effectively with anxious young people in the presence of their parents because the parents have so much more compassion for their children than regard for the honor of God. This is a position that is all wrong. If you hold such views and feelings, you are better off to hold your tongue than to say anything to the anxious.

I have often seen such cases. A mother will tell her anxious son he has always been a good, kind, and obedient child. Then she will beg him "not to carry on so" about the state of his soul.

A husband will tell his wife, or a wife her husband, "How good you are! Why, you are not so bad. You have been listening to that awful minister who frightens people, and now you are excited. Don't worry, I am sure you have not been bad enough to deserve such torment." But the truth is, they have been a great deal worse than they think they have been.

No sinner ever believes his sins are greater than they really are. No sinner ever has an adequate idea of how great a sinner he is. It is not likely that any man could live seeing the full picture of his sins. God has, in His mercy, spared all His creatures that worst of sights, a naked human heart.

Honesty _____

_____

_____

_____

_____

The sinner's guilt is deeper and more damning than he thinks, and his danger is much greater than he knows. If he were to see his sins as they are, he probably would not live one moment. Nonetheless, a sinner can have false ideas about the sin in his life. He may think he has committed the unpardonable sin, that he has grieved away the Spirit forever (see Matthew 12:32) or sinned away his day of grace. But telling the most moral and naturally amiable person in the world that he is good enough, that he is not as bad as he thinks, is not giving him rational comfort, but deceiving him and ruining his soul.

TRUE COMFORT FOR THE SINNER

The sinner is on the very verge of hell. He is in rebellion against God, and his danger is infinitely greater than he imagines. Oh, what a doctrine of devils (see 1 Timothy 4:1) it is to tell a rebel against heaven not to be worried! What is all his distress but rebellion itself? He is not comforted because he refuses to be comforted. God is ready to comfort him.

Do not think you must be more compassionate than God. He will fill the sinner with comfort immediately on submission. The sinner stands there struggling against God, the Holy Spirit, and conscience, until he is almost worried to death. Still he will not yield. Then someone will say, "Oh, I hate to see you feel so bad. Do not be so upset. Cheer up, cheer up! Christianity is not being gloomy. Don't fret!"

People sometimes comfort a sinner by telling him, "If you are one of Jesus' chosen few, you will be brought into His fold." I once heard of a young man experiencing great distress as he became aware of his sinful nature. He immediately went to see the neighboring minister about his problem. They talked for a long time.

As the young man was leaving, the minister said to him, "Please give this note to your father." His father was a good Christian. The minister wrote the letter and forgot to seal it. As the sinner was going home, he saw that the letter was not sealed, and he thought the minister probably had written about him. His curiosity led him to open the letter and read it.

And there he found words to this effect: "Dear Sir, I found your son under conviction and in great distress. It is not easy to say anything to give him relief. But if he is one of the Lord's chosen people, he will be saved."

He wanted to say something to comfort the father. But that letter nearly ruined the son's soul because he believed the doctrine of election, saying, "If I am elected, I will be brought in." His conviction of his sin was gone.

Years later, he was awakened and converted, but only after a great struggle, and not until that false impression had been obliterated from his mind. He was made to see that there was no salvation for him in the doctrine of election, and that, if he did not repent, he would be lost.

REFLECTION ON...

TRUE COMFORT _____

_____

_____

_____

_____

_____

INSTRUCTIONS TO CONVERTS

Feed My lambs.
—John 21:15

One of the first things young converts should be taught is to distinguish between emotion and principle in Christianity. Fix these words in your mind: distinguish between emotion and principle.

Emotion is the state of mind of which we are conscious and that we call feeling. It is an involuntary state of mind that arises under certain circumstances or certain influences. There may be intense feelings or tranquility, or feelings may disappear entirely. Principle is the voluntary decision of the mind, the firm determination to fulfill duty and to obey the will of God, by which a Christian should always be governed.

ACTING ON PRINCIPLE INSTEAD OF EMOTION

When a man decides to obey God because it is right, that is principle. Whether he feels any lively religious emotions at the time or not, he will do his duty cheerfully, readily, and heartily. This is acting out of principle and not emotion.

Many young converts have mistaken views on this subject. They let their feelings completely determine whether or not they will become involved in a Christian activity. Some will not lead a prayer meeting unless they feel they can pray an eloquent prayer.

Many are influenced almost entirely by their emotions. They give way to their feelings as if they felt they were under no obligation to duty unless urged on by some strong emotion. They will be very zealous in their beliefs when their emotions are warm and lively, but they will not act out their faith, consistently carrying it into every concern of life. They are religious only when they are impelled by a gush of feeling. This is not true religion.

REFLECTION ON...

EMOTION VERSUS PRINCIPLE _____

_____

_____

_____

_____

_____

AVOIDING SECTARIANISM

Young converts should not be influenced to be sectarian in their outlook. They should not be taught to dwell on denominational distinctions or to split hairs about doctrinal points. They should examine these points according to their importance, at a proper time and in a proper way. Then they should make up their minds for themselves. They should be taught not to dwell on them or make too much out of them, especially at the beginning of their religious lives.

When I hear a new believer asking, "Do you believe in the doctrine of election?" or "Do you believe in sprinkling?" or "Do you believe in immersing?" I feel sad. Young converts obsessed with such sectarian questions soon find that their zeal sours. This faultfinding eats out the heart of their religion and molds their entire characters into sinful, sectarian bigotry. They generally become extremely zealous for the traditions of the leaders, with little concern for the salvation of souls.

NONSECTARIANISM _____

_____

_____

_____

_____

ANSWERING THE CALL TO DUTY

Young converts should be carefully taught that when a task needs to be done, they are to do it. However dull your feelings may be, if duty calls, do it! Do not wait for feeling, just *do it!* Most likely, the very emotions you are waiting for will surface when you begin to do your duty.

If the duty is prayer, for instance, and you do not have the right feelings, do not wait for emotions before you pray. Pray and *"open your mouth wide"* (Psalm 81:10). By doing this, you are most likely to have the emotions you wanted, those that constitute the conscious happiness of religion.

SURRENDERING ALL TO GOD

Young converts need to be taught that they are neither owners of their possessions nor of themselves. Nothing is their own: their time, property, influence, faculties, body, or soul. *"You are not your own"* (1 Corinthians 6:19). They belong to God. When they submit to God, they surrender everything to Him, to be ruled and disposed of at His pleasure. Christians have no right to spend even one hour as if their time were their own. They really have no right to go anywhere or do anything for themselves. They should recognize that everything is at the disposal of God, and they must employ all for the glory of God.

The church and its Christian members must take a firm stance regarding stewardship, recognizing that denying responsibility here can be just as serious as denying the deity of Jesus. Everyone should also recognize that covetousness, fairly proved, can just as soon exclude a man from communion with Jesus as adultery.

It is time these matters were corrected. The only way to set Christians right is to begin with those who are just entering the Christian life. Young converts must be told that they are just as worthy of condemnation if they show a covetous spirit and turn a deaf ear when the whole world is calling for help as if they were living in adultery or practicing the daily worship of idols. Continuing like this would also exclude them from fellowship with the church.

PRAYING ALWAYS

Young converts should be taught always to pray, no matter what may take place. The lack of right instruction on this point causes many young converts to suffer loss and fall away from God.

For instance, a young convert will fall into sin and then feel as if he cannot pray. Instead of overcoming this barrier to prayer, he becomes so distressed that he waits for the pain of his distress to pass. Instead of going directly to Jesus Christ in the middle of his agony, confessing his sin out of the fullness of his heart, getting a renewed pardon and his peace restored, he waits until all of his affliction has subsided.

His repentance, then, if he does repent, is cold and half-hearted. Let me tell you, beloved, never do this. When your conscience presses you, go to Christ, confess your sin fully, and pour out your heart to God.

Sometimes people will neglect to pray because they are in the dark and feel no desire to pray. But that is the very time when they need prayer. That is the very reason they need to pray. You should go right to God and confess your coldness and darkness of mind. Tell Him just how you feel. Tell Him, "Lord, I have no desire to pray, but I know I should pray." Immediately the Spirit will come and lead your heart in prayer, and all the dark clouds will pass away.

LOOKING TO CHRIST ALONE
AS ONE'S MODEL

Young converts should be faithfully warned against adopting a false standard in religion. They should not be left to fall in behind old believers or see these Christians as a standard of holy living. They should always look at Christ as their model rather than at other Christians. They should aim to be holy. *"Be holy, for I am holy"* (1 Peter 1:16).

The church has been greatly hurt because of a lack of attention to this matter. Young converts have come forward with warm hearts and enough ardent zeal to aim for the highest standard. Yet because they were not properly directed, they soon decided that what was good enough for others was good enough for them. Therefore, they ceased to aim higher than those who were before them. And in this way, the church, instead of rising higher and higher in holiness with every revival, is kept nearly stationary.

CHRIST AS OUR PRIMARY MODEL

LEARNING TO SAY NO

Converts must learn to say no. This is a very difficult lesson for many. Perhaps a young woman loved the partying circle and loved its pleasures. Then she joined the church and found herself separated from all her old friends. Now they do not ask her to their concerts and parties because they know she will not join them. They may even keep away from her entirely for a while for fear she will talk with them about their souls.

But eventually, they will grow a little bold, and some of them may ask her to take a ride with a few friends. She would not like to say no. They are her old friends, only a few of them are going, and surely a ride is so innocent that she could accept the invitation. But now that she has begun to give in, the ice is broken, and they have her again as one of them. It goes on, and she begins to attend their social visits. "Only a few friends, you know." Finally, she may start staying out late again on Saturday nights and sleeping through church services on Sunday mornings. She may even miss a Communion service. All because she did not learn to say no.

Perhaps a young man was, for a time, always in Sunday school and at the prayer meeting. But his old friends begin to invite him to go out with them again, and they draw him away from the church, step by step. He reasons that, if he refuses to go with them in things that are innocent, he will lose his influence with them. And so he goes, until prayer meeting, Bible study, and even private Bible reading and prayer are neglected. Ah, young man, stop at the beginning! If you do not wish to expose the cause of Christ to scorn and contempt, learn to resist the beginnings of temptation.

REFLECTION ON...

SAYING NO _____

_____

_____

_____

_____

_____

BEING COMPLETELY HONEST

It is very important that young converts are taught to be strictly honest. This is very different from the world at large, and even different from most Christians. Unfortunately, how little conscience there is! How little of that real honesty, that pure, simple uprightness that ought to mark the life of a child of God there is!

Look at this seriously. Who does God say will go to heaven? Read Psalm 15 and see. *"He who swears to his own hurt and does not change"* (verse 4). What do you think of that? If a man has promised anything, except to commit sin, he must keep his promise if he wants to be honest and to go to heaven. But people will make promises, and because they cannot be prosecuted, they will then break them as if they were nothing. Yet they would not let a check of theirs be returned from the bank because they would lose credit.

Is this honest? Will this kind of honesty get them into heaven? Do you think you can carry a lie in your hand before God? (See Isaiah 44:20.) If you refuse or neglect to fulfill your promise, you are a liar. And if you persist in this, you risk going to hell. I would not, for anything, die with money in my hands that I had neglected to give as I had promised. Such money will *"spread like cancer"* (2 Timothy 2:17).

If you are unable to pay the money, you have a good excuse. But you are obligated to say so. If you refuse to pay what you have promised because you have changed your mind, you are guilty. You cannot pray until you pay that money. Will you pray, "Lord, I promised to give that money, but I changed my mind and broke my promise. Still, Lord, I ask You to bless me, although I keep my money. Make me happy in Your love"? Will such prayer be answered? Never!

DESIRING AND CHOOSING
THE RIGHT PATH

Christianity does not consist of mere *desires* to do good deeds. Desires that do not result in choice and action are not virtuous. Nor are such desires necessarily evil. They may arise involuntarily in the mind, in view of certain objects. But, while desires produce no voluntary act, they are no more virtuous or evil than the beating pulse.

The most wicked man on earth may have strong *desires* for holiness. He may clearly see that holiness is the only means of happiness. And the minute he understands that holiness is a means of happiness, he naturally desires it.

We can be concerned about the multitude of people who are deceiving themselves with the idea that simply a desire for holiness, as a means of happiness, is Christianity. Many people undoubtedly give themselves great credit for desires that never result in choosing right. They feel desire to do their duty, but do not choose to do it because they have even stronger desires not to do it. These desires are not noble. For an action or desire to be virtuous in the sight of God, it must be an act of the will.

People often talk most absurdly on this subject, as though their desires are good in themselves while they remain mere desires. "I think I desire to do so-and-so." But do you do it? "Oh no, but I often feel a desire to do it." This is practical atheism.

Whatever desires a person may have, if they are not carried out through actual choice and action, they are not virtuous. And no degree of desire is good within itself. If this idea could be made prominent, and fully riveted in the minds of men, it would probably annihilate the hopes of half the members of the church. This means all those who are living on their good desires, while doing nothing for God.

OBEYING GOD FROM THE HEART

Converts should be made to understand that nothing that is selfish is Christian. Whatever desires they may have, whatever choices and actions they may put forth, if the reason behind them is selfish, there is nothing faithful in them. A man may just as much commit sin in praying, reading the Bible, or going to a religious service as in anything else, if his motive is selfish.

Suppose a man prays with a view to simply promote his own happiness. Is that God-fearing? It is no more than attempting to make God his almighty servant! It is nothing but an attempt to put the universe and God in a position to make the self happy. It is the greatest degree of wickedness. It is so far from piety and goodness that it is superlative wickedness.

Nothing is acceptable to God, including religion, unless it is performed heartily to please God. No outward action has anything good unless it is performed with right motives and from the heart. Young converts should be taught fully and positively that loving Jesus is obeying God from the heart.

EXERCISING SELF-DENIAL

Christianity consists of voluntary action. Young converts must be taught that the duty of self-denial is one of the leading features of the gospel. They should understand that converts must be taught that they are no more faithful than they are willing to take up their crosses daily and deny themselves for Christ. (See Luke 9:23.)

There is little self-denial in the church, because such little instruction of this nature is given to young converts. How seldom are they told that self-denial is the leading feature in Christianity! In pleading for benevolent reasons, how often will you find that ministers and others do not even ask Christians to deny themselves for the sake of promoting their petitions! They ask them to give only what they can spare—in other words, to offer the Lord that which costs them nothing. What an abomination! Preachers ask only for the surplus, for what is not wanted, for what can as easily be given as not.

A PRAYER FOR...

Self-denial _____

_____

_____

_____

_____

_____

PRACTICING PERSEVERANCE

Young converts should be taught to understand what perseverance is. It is astonishing how people define perseverance. The true idea is that if a man is truly converted, he will, as a rule, *continue* to obey God despite difficulty and risk.

Obedience to God is in the state of the heart. It is being willing to obey God, willing to let God rule in all things. But if a man habitually disobeys God in any particular way, his state of mind renders obedience regarding anything else impossible. To say that in some things a man obeys God out of respect to His authority, and that in some other things, he refuses obedience, is absurd.

BEING TEMPERATE

Young converts can be easily taught to be *"temperate in all things"* (1 Corinthians 9:25). Yet this subject is greatly neglected in the teaching of young converts, and it is almost lost sight of in our churches. For example, chewing or smoking tobacco, even partaking of caffeine in coffee and tea, when there is no necessity for it, is intemperance. It is not being *"temperate in all things."*

Until Christians grow conscientious about this and learn that they have no right to be intemperate in anything, they will not make progress in their Christian walk.

How long will the church show a hypocritical face at the missionary meeting, asking God to save the world while throwing away five times as much for sheer intemperance as she will give to save the world? Some of you may think it is beneath the dignity of the pulpit to lecture against these things. But I tell you, it is a great mistake if you think these are little things. They make the church odious in the sight of God by exposing her hypocrisy and lust.

For example, an individual may pretend he has given himself up to serve Jesus Christ, yet refuse to deny himself any favorite lust. Then he will go and pray, "Lord, save the world; Lord, Your kingdom come!" This is hypocrisy. Will prayers like these be heard? Unless Christians are willing to deny themselves, using the money they spend on intemperance for missions, their prayers are not worth a penny.

These things must be taught to young converts. The church must not call people Christians unless they deny themselves for Christ's sake. Is this just a little thing? See how it poisons the spirit of prayer! Watch the lack of self-control debase the soul until it indulges in fleshly desires once again! Is it beneath the dignity of the pulpit to discuss stewardship when intemperate indulgences, of one kind and another, cost the church five if not fifty times more than all it gives for the salvation of the world?

Heaven calls from above, "Go...and preach the gospel to every creature" (Mark 16:15). Hell groans from beneath, and ten thousand voices cry out from heaven, earth, and hell, "Do something to save the world!" Do it now, or millions more will be in hell through your neglect. What right do you have to use Christ's money for your lusts? Are you a good steward? Be careful that you do not find out too late that you have preferred self-gratification above obedience. Be careful that no one can say about you: "Whose end is destruction, whose god is their belly, and whose glory is in their shame; who set their mind on earthly things" (Philippians 3:19).

The time to teach these things effectively is when converts are young. If converts are not properly taught in the beginning, they will start a wrong habit. They will begin with a self-indulgent mode of living, rarely becoming thoroughly reformed. I have conversed with longtime Christians on these subjects and have been astonished at their obstinacy in indulging their lusts. I am satisfied that the church can never rise out of sloth until young converts are faithfully taught, at the outset of their new lives, to be temperate in all things.

New Christians should be taught that they must be just as holy as they think ministers should be. For a long time, the idea has circulated that ministers must be holy and practice self-denial. And so they must. But it is strange that people would assume that ministers are bound to be holier than other people. These people would be shocked to see a minister using too much levity, being too fashion-conscious, or losing his temper.

Temperance _____

_____

_____

_____

_____

BEING PERFECT

Young converts should aim to be perfect.[3] They should be taught that if it is not their purpose to live without sin, they have not yet begun to be righteous. What is religion but a supreme love

___

3. This perfection is not absolute perfection, but perfection in love. —E. E. Shelhamer

for God and a supreme disposition to obey God? If these things are not there, there is no religion at all.

If any are prepared to say they are perfect, all I have to say is, "Let them prove it." If they are perfect, I hope they will show it by their actions.

Every Christian must strive to be perfect in motive. He must also strive for entire, perpetual, and universal obedience to God. It should be his constant purpose to live wholly for God and obey all His commandments. He should live so that if he were to sin, it would be an inconsistency, an exception. Christians should not sin at all. We are bound to be as holy as God is if we expect to live with Him one day. Young converts should be taught to start out in the right course, or they will never be right.

GOING FORWARD ALWAYS

When the young convert is rejoicing in his Savior, planning to live for the glory of God and the good of mankind, how often he is met with this reply: "You will not always feel so." Thus, his mind is prepared to expect to backslide and not to be surprised when he does. This is just what the devil wants young converts to hear from older Christians. "Your feelings will not last, and eventually you will be as cold as we are." It has made my heart bleed to see it!

When the new Christian has been pouring out his warm heart to some old believer, expecting the warm burstings of a kindred spirit to respond to his own, what does he encounter? This cold answer, coming like a northern blast over his soul, "You will not always feel like this." *Shame!*

The church is preparing the young convert to expect to backslide as a matter of course, so that when he begins to decline, he will not be alarmed. Under the very influences of this instruction, it is most likely he will look at it as a matter of course, doing as everybody else does.

This is the very last kind of doctrine that should be taught to young converts! They should be told that they have only begun the Christian life and that their faith will consist of going on in it. They should be taught to go forward all the time and grow in grace continually.

Do not teach them to taper off their religion, letting it grow smaller and smaller until it comes to a point. God says, *"The path of the just is like the shining sun, that shines ever brighter unto the perfect day"* (Proverbs 4:18). Now, whose path grows dimmer and dimmer unto the perfect night?

New Christians should be brought to such a state of mind that the first indications of decay in spirituality or zeal will alarm them and spur them up to duty. There is no need for young converts to backslide as they do. Paul did not backslide. And I do not doubt that this very doctrine, "You will not always feel so," is one of the grand devices of Satan to dampen the fire of the love of Jesus that a new Christian has.

REFLECTION ON...

BACKSLIDING _____

_____

_____

_____

_____

_____

BEING ENTIRELY CONSECRATED

The very idea of being a Christian is to renounce self and become entirely consecrated to God. A man has no more right to withhold anything from God than he has to rob or steal. It is robbery in the highest sense of the term. It is an infinitely higher crime than it would be for a clerk in a store to take his employer's money and spend it on his own lusts and pleasures.

I mean that for a man to withhold from God is a higher crime than what a man can commit against his fellowman. God is the Owner of all things in an infinitely higher sense than man can be the owner of anything.

If God calls on His people to employ anything they have—their money, time, children—or to dedicate themselves in advancing His kingdom, and they refuse, they are more to blame than if they embezzled their employer's money. Christians often fail here because they want things their own way, or they prefer to do something else.

DOING ONE'S WHOLE DUTY

Young converts should be taught to do all their duty. They should never make a compromise with duty or think of saying, "I will do this to offset neglecting that." They should never be satisfied until they have done their duties of every kind, in relation to their families, the church, Sunday schools, the impenitent around them, the disposal of their property, and the conversion of the world. Let everyone do his duty, as he feels it when his heart is warm. Never attempt to pick and choose among the commandments of God.

Teach young Christians that Christianity does not consist of raptures or ecstasies or high flights of feeling. There may be a great deal of these where there is religion. But it should be understood that these are all involuntary emotions and can exist in full power where there is no religion. These feelings may be the mere workings of the imagination, without any truly religious affection at all. People may have them to such an extent that they actually swoon with ecstasy—even on the subject of religion—without having any religion. I have known people to be carried away with rapture by a mere view of the natural attributes of God, His power and wisdom as displayed in the starry heavens. Yet these people are not Christians. Christianity is obedience to God, the voluntary submission of the soul to His will.

A NEW CONVERT _____

_____

_____

_____

_____

_____

BE FILLED WITH THE SPIRIT

Be filled with the Spirit.
—Ephesians 5:18

Why do many people not have the Spirit? It may be that they live a hypocritical life. Their prayers are not earnest and sincere. Not only is their religion a mere show without any heart, but they are insincere in their personal exchanges with others.

Others are so frivolous that the Spirit will not dwell with them.

Others are so proud that they cannot have the Spirit. They like to find ways to prove to everyone that they are better than others. They are so fond of dress, high life, and fashion, it is no wonder they are not filled with the Spirit.

Some are so worldly-minded, love property so much, and are trying so hard to get rich that they cannot have the Spirit. How can He dwell with them when all their thoughts are on things of the world and all their powers are absorbed in procuring wealth? And when they get money, they are in agony if their consciences pressure them to do something with it for the conversion of the world.

They show how much they love the world in all their conversations with others. Little things show it. They will badger a poor man who is doing a little piece of work for them down to the lowest penny. But if they are dealing on a large scale, very likely they will be liberal and fair because it is for their advantage.

If they do not care about the person—a laborer, mechanic, or servant—they will grind him down to the last fraction, no matter what his work is really worth. They actually pretend to make it a matter of conscience that they cannot possibly give any more. Now, they would be ashamed to deal like this with people of their own rank because it would be found out and injure their reputations.

But God knows it and has it all written down. He knows they are covetous and unfair in their dealings. He knows they will not do right as a matter of course, but only when it is for their interest. Now, how can such believers have the Spirit of God? It is impossible.

Others are neglecting some known duty, and that is why they do not have the Spirit. For example, perhaps a man is not praying with his family, though he knows he should, but is trying to get the spirit of prayer!

If you have neglected any known duty and lost the spirit of prayer, you must yield first. God has a disagreement with you. You have refused obedience to God, and you must change. You may have forgotten it, but God has not. You must recall your failure and repent. God never will yield or grant you His Spirit until you repent.

If you know what it is to commune with God, how sweet it is to dissolve in penitence and to be filled with the Spirit, you cannot help but desire a return of those joys. You may determine to pray earnestly for them and to pray for a revival of religion. But, on the whole, you are unwilling to see these things come. You have so much to do that you cannot wait for them.

Or revival would require so many sacrifices that you cannot bear to have it. There are some things you are not willing to give up. You find that, if you wish to have the Spirit of God dwell with you, you must lead a different life. You must give up the world. You must make sacrifices. You must break off from your worldly associations and confess your sins. So, on the whole, you do not really want to have the Spirit come, unless He will consent to let you live as you please. He will never do that.

Yielding_____

_____

_____

_____

_____

Your guilt is as great as the authority of God that commands you, *"Be filled with the Spirit."* God commands it, and refusing to do so would be just as much a disobedience of God's commands as swearing, stealing, committing adultery, or breaking the Sabbath. Yet there are many people who do not blame themselves at all for not having the Spirit. They even think they are very good Christians because they go to prayer meetings and take

Communion, though they live year after year without the Spirit of God. God who says, *"Do not be drunk"* (Ephesians 5:18) also says, *"Be filled with the Spirit."*

You say that if a man is a habitual adulterer or a thief, he is no Christian. Why? Because he lives in habitual disobedience to God. Likewise, if he swears, you have no love for him. You will not allow him to plead that his heart is right and that words are nothing. He cannot tell you that God does not care about words. You would think it outrageous to have such a man in the church or to have a group of these people pretend to call themselves a Christian church. Yet they are no more living in disobedience to God than you are, you who live without the spirit of prayer and without the presence of God.

Your guilt is equal to all the good you might do if you were filled with the Spirit of God in as great a measure as it is your duty to be. You are entirely responsible to the church and to God for all this good that you might do. A man is responsible for all the good he can do.

REFLECTION ON...

Your responsibility _____

_____

_____

_____

_____

_____

If you are filled with the Spirit, you will be called eccentric, and you will probably deserve it. Probably you really will be eccentric. I never knew a person who was filled with the Spirit who was not called eccentric. The reason is that such people are unlike other people. They act under different influences, take different views, are moved by different motives, and are led by a different Spirit. You are to expect such remarks.

I have often heard this remark regarding such a person: "He is a good man, but he is rather eccentric." I have sometimes asked for specifics. How is he eccentric? Their answer amounts to this: he is spiritual. Make up your mind to be "eccentric." There is such a thing as false eccentricity, and it is horrible! But there is such a thing as being so deeply imbued with the Spirit of God that you must and will appear strange and eccentric to those who cannot understand the reasons behind your conduct.

Paul was accused of being deranged by those who did not understand the power under which he acted. No doubt, Festus thought he was crazy, that *"much learning"* had driven him mad (Acts 26:24). But Paul said, *"I am not mad,…but speak the words of truth and reason"* (verse 25). His conduct was so strange, so novel, that Festus thought it must be insanity. But the truth simply was that Paul saw spiritual things so clearly that he threw his whole soul into them. You must make up your mind to do the same thing, and increasingly so, the more you live apart from the world and walk closer to God.

RENEWAL NEEDED AMONG THE CLERGY

The piety of the ministry, though real, is so superficial, in many instances, that the spiritual people of the church feel that ministers do not and cannot sympathize with them.

This evil is one of the worst that we are experiencing today. The preaching does not meet the congregation's needs. It does not feed them. The ministers do not have enough depth of religious experience to know how to search and wake up the church, help those under temptation, support the weak, and direct the strong.

When a minister has gone with a church as far as his experience in spirituality goes, he stops. Until he has a renewed experience, until his heart has been broken up afresh and starts again in the divine life and Christian experience, he will not help his congregation further. He may preach sound doctrine, but so can an unconverted minister. His preaching will lack that searching pungency, that practical bearing, that anointing that alone will reach the spiritually minded Christian.

It is a fact (over which the church is groaning) that the piety of young people suffers so much during the course of their education that, when they enter the ministry, however much intellectual maturity they may possess, they are spiritual babies. They need nursing; they need to be fed. Consequently, they are unable to feed the church of God.

A PRAYER FOR...

Ａｌｌ　ｓｐｉｒｉｔｕａｌ　ｌｅａｄｅｒｓ　_____

_____

_____

_____

_____

_____

ACCEPTING THE REALITY OF CONFLICT

From the Church

If you are filled with the Spirit of God, you must accept the fact that you will experience opposition, both in the church and in the world.

Very likely, the leading men in the church will oppose you. There has always been opposition in the church. It was this way when Christ was on earth. If you are far above their state of feeling, church members will oppose you. *"Yes, and all who desire to live godly in Christ Jesus will suffer persecution"* (2 Timothy 3:12). Often the elders and even the minister will oppose you if you are filled with the Spirit of God.

From Satan

You must expect very frequent and agonizing conflicts with Satan. Satan has very little trouble with Christians who are not spiritual, but are instead lukewarm, slothful, and worldly minded. These Christians do not understand what is said about spiritual conflicts. Perhaps they will smile when spiritual battles are mentioned. So the devil leaves them alone. They do not disturb him, nor he them.

But spiritual Christians, whom Satan understands very well, are really injuring him; therefore, he sets himself against them. Such Christians often have terrible conflicts. They have temptations that they never dreamed of before: blasphemous thoughts, atheistic ideas, suggestions to do deeds of wickedness, to destroy their own lives, and more. If you are spiritual, you can expect these terrible conflicts.

Within Yourself

You will have greater conflicts within yourself than you ever dreamed of. You will sometimes find your own weaknesses making strange headway against the Spirit. *"The flesh lusts against the Spirit, and the Spirit against the flesh"* (Galatians 5:17). Such a Christian (until wholly sanctified) is often thrown into consternation at the power of his own corruptions.

CONFLICT _____

_____

_____

_____

_____

_____

FINDING PEACE AMID CONFLICT

But you will have peace with God. If the church, sinners, and the devil oppose you, there will be One with whom you will have peace. Let you who are called to these trials, conflicts, and temptations, and you who groan, pray, weep, and break your hearts, remember this consideration. Your peace toward God will flow like a river. You will also have peace of conscience if you are led by the Spirit. You will not be constantly goaded and tortured by a guilty conscience. Your conscience will be as calm, quiet, and unruffled as a lake in summer.

BEING USEFUL IN THE SPIRIT

If you are filled with the Spirit, you will be useful. You cannot help being useful. Even if you were sick and unable to leave your room and could see no one, you would be ten times more useful than a hundred lukewarm Christians with no spirituality.

Once a fine Christian man was dying of tuberculosis. He was poor and had been sick for years. A very kind, but unconverted, merchant in town would send him things for his comfort and for his family. The dying man was grateful for the kindness, but he could not return the favor.

Finally, he decided that praying for the merchant's salvation was the greatest gift he could give. He began to pray. His soul kindled with the Spirit, and he was in vibrant communication with God.

At that time, there was not a revival in progress, but to everyone's astonishment, the merchant accepted Jesus as his Lord. This spark kindled the roaring fire of revival all over town, and many, many people were saved.

This poor man lingered in a condition of weakness for several years. After his death, I visited his home, and his widow showed me his diary. Among other entries was this: "I am acquainted with about thirty ministers and churches." He went on to say how he set aside certain hours in the day and week to pray for each of these ministers and churches. He also prayed for different missionary stations.

Generally, his diary read like this: "Today I was enabled to offer what I call the prayer of faith for the outpouring of the Spirit on ——— church, and I trust God will soon bring a revival." On another date, he wrote, "I have today been able to offer what I call the prayer of faith for ——— church, and trust there will be a revival there." Thus he prayed over a great number of churches, recording the fact that he prayed for them in faith that a revival would soon start among them.

Of the missionary stations, he mentioned in particular one at Ceylon. I believe the last place mentioned in his diary for which he offered the prayer of faith was the place in which he lived. Not long after, revival started in each of the places mentioned in his diary, nearly in the order in which they were mentioned. In due time, news came from Ceylon that revival was in progress there.

However, the revival in his own town did not start until after his death. It started the moment his widow gave me the documents to which I have referred. She told me that he prayed so much during his sickness that she often feared he would "pray himself to death."

The revival was great and powerful in the whole region, and the fact that it was about to start was not hidden from this dying servant of the Lord. According to God's Word, *"The secret of the LORD is with those who fear Him"* (Psalm 25:14). Thus, this man, too feeble in body to leave his house, was more useful to the world and the church than all the lukewarm believers in the country.

BEING USEFUL

EXEMPLIFYING CHRIST'S CHARACTER

If you are filled with the Spirit, you will not find yourself distressed, annoyed, or worried when people speak against you. When I find people irritated and fretting over every little thing that touches them, I am sure they are not filled with the Spirit of Christ. Jesus Christ could have everything said against Him that malice invented, and yet not be disturbed by it. If you desire to be meek under persecution, to exemplify the temper of the Savior, and to honor religion in this way, you need to be filled with the Spirit.

You will be calm under affliction. You will not be confused or worried when you see a storm coming. People will be astonished at your calm and cheerful disposition under heavy trials. They will not understand the inner support Spirit-filled believers have.

CHRIST'S CHARACTER _____

_____

_____

_____

_____

_____

USING WISDOM IN THE CONVERSION OF SINNERS

If you are filled with the Spirit, you will be wise in your use of means for the conversion of sinners. The Spirit will lead you to use these means wisely, in a way adapted to accomplish their purposes and to avoid doing any harm.

HAVING A CHILDLIKE SPIRIT

If you do not have the Spirit, you will very likely stumble because of those who do. You will doubt the propriety of their conduct. If they seem to feel things a good deal more than you do, you will likely call this "base feeling." You will perhaps doubt their sincerity when they say they have these feelings. You will say, "I don't know what to think of so-and-so. He seems to be very pious, but I do not understand him. I think he has a lot of base feeling." You will be trying to criticize them to justify yourself.

If you want to have the Spirit, you must be childlike and yield to His influences. If He is drawing you to prayer, you must stop everything to yield to His gentle strivings. No doubt, you have sometimes felt a desire to pray for something, and you have put it off and resisted until God finally stopped calling you. If you wish Him to remain, you must yield to His softest leadings, watch and learn what He wants you to do, and yield yourself to His guidance.

THE PRESENCE OF THE SPIRIT REQUIRES SACRIFICE

Christians should be willing to make any sacrifice in order to enjoy the presence of the Spirit. Once a wealthy Christian woman said, "I must either stop listening to this preacher or give up my love for the extravagant life." She gave up listening to the preacher.

However, another wealthy woman heard the Word of the Lord from the same preacher. She, too, was a believer, but she chose to place more importance on Jesus than worldly things. Her whole approach to life changed, so that she spent more time in communion with God and doing good deeds.

You see from this example that it can be very difficult for wealthy people to go to heaven. What a tragedy it would be if we kept a circle of friends who loved living the wild life. Such people are missing so much. Who can enjoy the presence of God with them?

Therefore, brethren, be even more diligent to make your call and election sure, for if you do these things you will never stumble; for so an entrance will be supplied to you abundantly into the everlasting kingdom of our Lord and Savior Jesus Christ. (2 Peter 1:10–11)

Revival today _____

_____

_____

_____

_____

_____

IN CONCLUSION

What is your definition of revival after finishing this book?

_____

_____

_____

_____

_____

_____

What have you read that will help you spark revival in your own life?

_____

_____

_____

_____

_____

_____

_____

_____

Where do you think you might see revival in your lifetime?

_____

_____

_____

_____

_____

_____

_____

_____

_____

_____

_____

_____

_____

_____

_____

_____

_____

"A revival is nothing else
than a new beginning of obedience to God."
—*Charles Finney*

Welcome to Our House!

We Have a Special Gift for You ...

It is our privilege and pleasure to share in your love of Christian classics by publishing books that enrich your life and encourage your faith.

To show our appreciation, we invite you to sign up to receive a specially selected **Reader Appreciation Gift**, with our compliments. Just go to the Web address at the bottom of this page.

God bless you as you seek a deeper walk with Him!

WE HAVE A GIFT FOR YOU

whpub.me/classicthx

WHITAKER
HOUSE